WARNING

POTHOLES, NEXT 9600KM

WARNING

POTHOLES, NEXT 9600KM

Contemplating Life After Birth

CAROL ANNE TUCKER

authorHOUSE®

AuthorHouse™
1663 Liberty Drive
Bloomington, IN 47403
www.authorhouse.com
Phone: 1-800-839-8640

First published by AuthorHouse   08/10/2011

ISBN: 978-1-4567-8281-8 (sc)

Printed in the United States of America

Any people depicted in stock imagery provided by Thinkstock are models, and such images are being used for illustrative purposes only.
Certain stock imagery © Thinkstock.

This book is printed on acid-free paper.

Because of the dynamic nature of the Internet, any web addresses or links contained in this book may have changed since publication and may no longer be valid. The views expressed in this work are solely those of the author and do not necessarily reflect the views of the publisher, and the publisher hereby disclaims any responsibility for them.

THIS BOOK IS DEDICATED TO:

JESUS CHRIST
For everything You ever did for each one of us
Long before any of this began.

JAMIE ACE
Thank you for taking such good care of us in both
Richer and poorer, sickness and health
Better and worse.
Our lives are richer, healthier and better because of it.

TO MY CHILDREN
For teaching me so much, for all your love and support,
You are always blessings and a joy to us
No matter what.

TO DAD AND MUZ
Both of you for believing in this project and
All your encouragement
Dad for the cartoons and how much fun
We had putting them together

FOREWORD

Meeting Carol Tucker is meeting a lady. She doesn't talk much; her writing gives all the expressions of her heart. I thoroughly enjoyed reading her book, as it was really getting to know Carol in the most practical way. Her true story of the Rhodesian lifestyle and the subsequent bush war paints pictures that you can clearly see. I can taste the dust and hear the cries of the birds and it is so real. The heartache of the people portrayed in her life is poignant and the characters that shaped her existence are memorable.

Being South African I knew of the 'troubles' north. The depth of this narrative is so relevant today as we still look with horror at what is happening in Zimbabwe and this where the true power of this book is. Jesus is glorified and all through this story there is the magnificence of his Grace interwoven through the tapestry of the stories, lives, circumstances and heart breaking traumas. I have had Grace explained by many theologians, preachers and teachers but never that it has become so engrained in my life, in my heart, as Carol has explained it.

She also said 'if life gives you lemons, don't grumble, make lemonade!' This book cannot be put down and when you read to the end, your overwhelming feeling, is a sense of joy. Even when things are not right in the world, GOD is still on his throne and you are never alone.

The dual purpose of the book is to encourage people to get to know Jesus as their personal savior and just as importantly to help every wavering Christian reading this book. We all go through trials, temptations and tribulations. Carol has encapsulated what Jesus was on earth here to do was to have a direct channel to GOD, and how to live your life victoriously here on earth, in Satan's territory.

Carol has such a lovely twinkle in her bright blue eyes and it is reflected in her humour in the book. We all love a good laugh and I know that Jesus had a tremendous sense of humour because we are all made in his image.

Read onwards dear friend and you will be blessed by all the little nuggets of love, life, family and the amazing story of why Jesus loves us so much. As Carol so rightly says, we will leave a wonderful fragrance of the Lord wherever we go, as we keep him close in our hearts.

No one can foresee the future and what will happen in Zimbabwe. The story will be told in years to come. What we can do is pray, that the people of that wonderful country will know GOD'S GRACE and that this book will be a Lighthouse of GOD'S abundant mercy.

Grant Camilleri
Author of: THE ETERNAL LIGHT

INTRODUCTION

All human beings will experience some suffering in their lives. Rarely—very rarely—does someone manage to sail on through from the heady and exciting days of *Blue Lagoon* to the mellow years of *On Golden Pond*, enjoying untroubled waters all the way. Sudden squalls, storms, doldrums, blistering heat, freezing cold, and the like will mar the journey from time to time. Many times we hear the words: It is not the circumstances that are the problem, but how we allow them to affect us and how we deal with them that truly count towards making us stronger, better and more capable people; in other words, people of strong, mature character.

The calm, clear, warm and sunny days are there for our enjoyment, but they do not make us grow strong. If you're like me, then chances are you'd just end up a happy little *sissie,* and maybe like me, you'd really prefer it that way. But Africa is not a place for *sissies* and none of the bibles 'Heroes of Faith' were *sissies* either.

Pain can sometimes be caused by loss of expectations. Imagine an athlete, or sportsman training for months for a particular contest, only to have to withdraw through injury at the last moment.

Then there comes a time in everyone's life when they realize that hopes, dreams and goals which emerged in youth, will never actually come to realization. Most of us will dream dreams, which are bigger and more elaborate than those that we actually are capable of achieving; letting go can be hard.

We have to accept that we are no longer young and that certain physical disciplines are now beyond our reach forever and that means letting go. Putting away rugby boots, ice skating boots or squash and tennis racquets for the last time heralds the end of an era. For some people the mid-life crisis can be very traumatic, and may take time and even counseling before acceptance is reached.

All of us must expect to lose a loved one at some point in our lives. Especially if events follow their natural course, then our parents will pass on before us, leaving an empty space behind them. Friends and family members may die from illness or injury. Each time, we must pass through the valley of the shadow of death, and walk through the grieving cycle, until we reach the 'door of hope' at the other side.

There are many other forms of suffering. The list is endless, and I cannot possibly describe them all without coming dangerously close to expressing a kind of underlying hopelessness over the plight of mankind and that is not my intention. Rather it was the way Almighty God brought me through each and every one that I want to share. I remember reading the *'Good News for Modern Man'* bible as a teenager and how excited I was to discover that all we needed was to believe in Jesus in order to be given eternal life—nothing else was required! No effort on our part at all. No going out and earning credits.

Now that was some amazing declaration for a sovereign God to make! But from that moment of realization onwards, the journey of faith became difficult, even fraught as God used many incidents and losses, people with strong faith and those with none at all to test that faith again and again. And when I thought I'd reached the end of my limit, He tested it some more. His joy has become my strength, the priceless gift of humour that lifted me above the pain on many occasions. So if I use humour to offset pain and suffering, it is because I am qualified enough to do this. It isn't a shallow attempt to spread 'sweetness and light' and kiss the wounds so that they feel okay. I know better than to try and do that. In His eyes, in our times of greatest trials are also times when He provides us with His heavenly robes. All of heaven's resources are at our disposal and that is the greatest gift of all—provided you simply believe. And over the years, I've come to understand what the true meaning of 'repentance' actually is. It's difficult to preach 'only believe' without adding something about 'repentance' in your message, so understanding what repentance truly is, is vital to your message.

Some forms of suffering I would classify as 'subnormal'. As with most things in life, it is not exactly a totally black-and-white issue, there must always be some gray areas—but some things just should not happen to anyone.

It is not 'normal' for a country's government to turn on the sector of its population who provide the baseline for most of its economy and destroy them using violence, terror, oppression and intimidation. Whatever reasons anyone may find in favour of 'land reform' in Zimbabwe there were ways of accomplishing the task without resorting to such underhanded tactics to achieve it. Nothing that has happened in the past can ever justify what has happened and the terrible suffering involved.

There is another kind of suffering that is also very hard for anyone to deal with and that is the kind which results in poor choices, mistakes, addictions; the kind for which for whatever reason, we ourselves are responsible for the suffering unleashed. Reaching out to someone in such a position for Jesus can be so difficult because so often they cannot believe Jesus would be interested in loving them or helping them.

Yet He was! He was the most moral man who ever lived but the sinners of His day; the publicans and prostitutes, tax collectors, those deemed 'unclean' and sinners were drawn to Him and He spent a great deal of time with Him. He had a clear message of unconditional love, forgiveness and healing for them. The bible calls it 'grace'—some say that GRACE is God's Riches At Christ's Expense.

But true as that statement may be, it can sometimes sound a little too spiritual for its simple, every day application. I like to think of this grace as 'Jesus at Work' and His people enjoying the benefits. He does for us all of that which we cannot do for ourselves. Grace is taking away all our sins, our shame, our guilt and wiping the slate forever clean. And then He imputes His very own righteousness into our accounts—a righteousness we clearly cannot earn and will never deserve. His salvation is like an undergarment; His righteousness is like an outer garment, or robe (not bathrobe—royal robe).

All this Jesus achieved with His life, death, resurrection and ascension.

We are King's Kids, double *Whoopah!* Epic *Whoopah!* His bible is a rich storehouse of priceless treasure that we can go romping through regularly and often.

He'll make us 'Fishers of Men' and if we'll just 'catch' them, He'll 'clean' them. That's grace and morality in its proper order of priority. The Kingdom of God is a party—it's a *Come As You Are* party. Just be honest about who you are to Jesus—He likes it better that way.

Against this background of grief, despair and trauma, there were always positive aspects, priceless pearls of wisdom plus coping skills and an ever-deepening understanding of God's empowering grace that helped us overcome. The close ties we formed with others, the caring and sharing which took place in the community, the Zimbabwean sense of humour—the one we relied on to help us keep an even keel even in some of life's darkest moments. Sooner or later most of us get to ask Him one form or another of that great, unanswered but nevertheless universal question: the *why's* of undeserved suffering. Like Job, there may an astounding answer for it, or like Habakkuk there may be one that we couldn't possibly understand from this earthly perspective.

The way we had understood and learned to trust God changed greatly, and our faith did grow stronger as we began to depend completely on Him for everything; for the very gift of life, strengthened and perfected in the Hard School of Learning itself and everything else which stems from that. Then He gave us His strength—the eternal Wings of Joy that lifted us up and taught us how to fly.

Each chapter holds a brief account of this story. At the end of each chapter are the 'Potholes: Below the Surface' priceless pearls of wisdom that the Lord taught us through the hardships. They are for those who, like all good ducks, like to dip below the surface of His eternal word and seek the deep things He likes to teach us. This is followed by 'Potholes: Short Thoughts' passages—something short and simple to brighten your day and help keep you focused. Finally comes the 'Potholes: Joy Bug'—that whizzy little firefly that lights up the ever-deepening gloom of night, livening life up and imparting JOY and the strength that comes with it.

CHAPTER ONE

'Those were the days my friend,
We thought they'd never end . . .'

So went that old song of yesteryear and a popular song in my childhood. I do not recall who the singer was, or most of the song, but wryly smile at the sentiment expressed. Those were the days, and yes, there was a time when we thought they were endless.

My grandparents' farm lay in a long peninsula of lush farmland and savannah bushveld east of Fort Victoria. The valley was tucked into a meandering line of indigo hills, and *Rippling Waters* was, for my sister Melanie (or Melan) and me was simply the best place in the world. It seemed an endless drive from Salisbury—around five hours if Dad was driving but closer to four if Mum was singing at the wheel. Whichever way, though, we'd usually arrive late afternoon. In the slanting rays of hot sunshine, the dust shone red-gold. Like an old friend, the huge farmyard held the welcoming joy of familiarity with its barns, pigsties, duck pond and workshops was full of the rich earthy smells of domestic animals and livestock, various stock feeds, molasses and diesel fumes from the tractors all of which silently invited us to explore, explore, explore.

If we arrived after the boiler had been lit, then the sharp, fragrant tang of wood smoke would be there to greet us too. The African labour force was always chattering loudly, often at the same time, with no apparent need for anyone to listen. Four thousand acres in which to farm 700 head of cattle and fields of maize, cotton and sorghum for the Grandparents, and four thousand acres of playground heaven for us, including savannah bush, acacia thornveld, huge, steep msasa-stippled 'gomos', dams of opaque red water after the annual rains.

We explored every inch of it, time and again, usually barefoot. You had to get hold of your environment. Not just sight and sound, but touch and smell as well. The best way to do that was to leave your 'takkies'

1

home and go barefoot. Scootching through dew-damp grass and leaving 'giant's footprints' being chased by the golden rays of sunshine, and surrounded by the glad outpourings of the thunderous dawn chorus, was pure heaven—aside from the liberal smatterings of paper thorns which we tried, without success, to avoid.

Every morning, when the early chores of feeding the livestock and poultry and milking the dairy cattle were completed we could sit down to the citrus zing of a huge pile of farm-grown fruit straight from the orchard, then porridge, bacon and eggs, toast and tea. Since the chores happened first, though, a good wash was required before entering the dining room. Otherwise outside smells of cow, chicken, duck, feed or diesel could sneak into the room behind you and that was unacceptable to the adults, sadly. Pig sty and Matabele Ant were two smells that were too noticeable to sneak anywhere.

'Who has been playing Stink the Ant?' Dad would ask in a tone that sent us scuttling out again for a retry at washing in a cream-and-green, queen-sized bathroom that smelt of Lifebouy and Haze Air Freshener.

Technically, we did have four seasons: Almost Summer, Summer, Still Summer and Christmas. Sometimes, though, a cool and grey misty drizzle we called 'guti' would creep up from the south, and if anything that meant a whole lot more exploration could be achieved without the usual heat exhaustion. Being barefoot a lot means that at a young age, we were expert on all species of thorns, but I have a feeling that most of the names we gave them, 'cow horn thorns' and 'devil thorns' were of our own making. The long white acacia thorns were the worst, causing an awful burning sensation that lasted for hours and a wound that sometimes went septic.

Many evenings we had to lay stomach-down, nose-to-pile on Gran's luxurious red and gold Axminster lounge carpet listening to the painful wheezing and crackling of static on the radio which muffled and distorted the six o'clock news and Muz (affectionate nickname for my mother) dug thorns out of our feet with a needle.

'Jeez, where have you been exploring today? Just look at the size of this,' she'd say, holding up the needle with a long, black, nasty-looking spike hanging wickedly off the end.

'Outside,' I'd mumble apologetically admiring the neat holes left behind in my feet.

Exploring a farm in Africa in that way brought its daily round of hazards, like snakes, wild pig, porcupines and other scary wildlife, sometimes rabid scary animals necessitating the use of weapons of some kind. Rabies was a continual threat with two phases: 'dumb-babies' in which the animal had no real conscious awareness of its surrounds, blindly stumbling around in a baffled daze, but also the more dangerous 'furious' stage in which they would snarl, snap and attack virtually anything.

'If you're going out and about, you do need some form of self defense and weapons are probably the best,' Dad informed us one day probably becoming more concerned about us meeting wild *people* in the bush. Young white girls in the wilds of Africa may well encounter other hazards as well. Melan spat out half a dozen or so 'Marksman' lead pellets into a grubby hand.

'We got this one,' she said, affectionately patting the gleaming steel-blue barrel of the BSA *Meteorite* with the other.

'No. I'm thinking bigger than that.'

He took Melan and me to the secret out-of-bounds Chamber of the Gun Cabinet. The locking mechanism was stiff and it took a few moments to pry open, making the waiting unbearable. Once it did, the rank smell of gun oil seeped out into the room and inside the dark interior of the cabinet was an array of deadly-looking rifles and a couple of squatty hand guns. Dad selected two: the .410 shotgun and the .22 rifle. He reached to the top shelf where various boxes of ammunition were stored and stuffed an assortment into his pockets.

A long, long safety lecture followed; the result of which we never aimed a weapon at anything we did not intend to kill. Guns were loaded only when necessary and if the shot was not taken, then they were unloaded again. A perfect safety record was the result. Once Dad was satisfied, then we took the rifles and a red net bag of rotten and discoloured gem squash to a rocky outcrop. Impressive weapons—one made a small, neat hole in the gem squash, the other pulverized it, leaving splatted gem squash all over the scenery.

'So, in conclusion, if you want to eat something after you've shot it, the .22 is better,' said Dad. 'Then again, depending on your aim, if you want to hit it at all the .410 gives you more scope. Guinea fowl make excellent running targets if you become a Marksman of Note, but they are notoriously difficult to hit.'

Grandpa had other weapons, too. One was an old Winchester rifle, complete with saddle ring; and a beautiful but heavy double-barrel shotgun amongst others. Dad usually used the Winchester and Grandpa took the double-barrel shotgun and outings with these accoutrements made the pickup look like a spiked porcupine.

Grandpa had a metal bar welded to the top of the pickup truck so that we could stand at the back, hold onto the bar with one hand and keep the big rifles upright slung over the other shoulder. Thus in the early mornings we'd set off in the damp mist as the sun rose over the horizon into the lands singing loudly and occasionally waving to cars whizzing past on the main road. The large herds of cattle needed plenty of attention so we'd take huge bags of molasses-laden feed to them. The sweet smell of molasses was almost appetizing, especially once hunger pangs kicked in but the feed also contained a small quantity of urea which is toxic to humans thus ensuring it was never that tempting.

Somehow the cattle knew when we came bearing stock feed and they'd come bellowing and crashing through the bush at a run, apparently anxious to get hold of it. Looking back I wonder how we handled those huge, jostling bovines with such total lack of fear, pushing them out the way so that we could load the feed into the big drums placed there for that purpose.

Out of all those cattle, there was only one animal, a Jersey bull named Warren, who was bad tempered anyway but who developed a chronic spite for Grandpa for no known reason, always chasing him away from the dairy herd. He was never a threat to us, but Grandpa had to keep his distance from that wily old bull.

Every week we'd take truckloads of African labourers to round the cattle all up and herd them back to the spray race for 'dip day' and other cattle-related issues; branding, dehorning, and castrating. Melan and I were allowed to participate in all of it, except the castration. Grandpa, being an 'olde worlde' type gentleman refused to allow his young granddaughters to either watch or participate in this particular chore.

I remember well graduation day onto the most prized weapon of all—the lethal-looking Colt 45. Dad got some charcoal, carefully and artistically drawing a man-sized target onto cardboard, setting it up on an embankment to approximate what it might be like to shoot at a real person. I fired two shots, and when the thunderous roar that bolted my eardrums together and the acrid smell of cordite had all subsided, I opened my eyes and looked at the target. The aim was true and both bullets had ripped into the cardboard man, one in the kidney region and the other where no man would ever want to get shot. 'Well,' said Dad dryly surveying the damage, 'with one shot he would be dead and the other he would just *wish* he was dead.'

They were days of total freedom and full of experiences and learning so many things; like checking various features on a bird so that you could accurately identify it. It was thus that I discovered a yellow-bellied sunbird, not previously recorded in any area other than Inyanga.

The epicentre of Gran's garden was a huge old wild fig tree, where numerous brightly-coloured fruit-eating birds would gather: the hippy-like speckled barbets, the thrilling, shimmering purple radiance of the plum-coloured starlings, and the cheery, cheeky 'pick puck peeka jock' of the bulbuls (more commonly known as 'toppies') could be seen on any day.

Then there were the green pigeons and mouse birds that'd fly in for a gorge on the fruit and fly straight out again, dawn and dusk, without fail. How I loved those green pigeons with their harsh barking calls and their glorious mish-mash of olive greens, misty grays and soft mauves, blending harmoniously with hectic slashes of rich scarlet and bright yellow. It was as though God had taken His palette of colours and just had a lot of fun sloshing various colours onto these big birds and yet making them blend perfectly as only a Mighty Hand at work could do. The midday heat was often broken by the continuous metallic clink of the yellow-fronted tinker-barbet, a shy bird that we rarely saw. Red-collared widow-birds and whydahs dotted the bushveld in summer. The glamorous males, with their bright colours and long black tails seemed to have difficulty flying and used to reach no more than top-of-the-veldt-grass height. I was always sure we could catch one, but we never did.

I learned the hard way that tractors have a different acceleration system to pickup trucks and their brakes are hard to engage. Careering towards the boiler (the only source of hot water on the entire farm) wasn't a great time to discover your ineptitude with the brakes.

Thanks to Bill (Muz' younger brother and our uncle) we learned how to blow birds' eggs without squashing the delicate shells, make raincoats out of fertilizer bags and also that the inside hollow of kudu horns smell putrid. Just one experimental sniff will have you retching and reeling. He taught us other things too; things that took me many years to *unlearn*. Just for the record, woodlice are not 'purple people eaters'—they have never attempted to eat live people. Corn crickets (which for some inexplicable reason we renamed 'obrom boop-pants') do not grow an extra leg so that they can eat one when they are hungry. There is no such thing as a 'Vooping Bird' who spends its days 'vooping' unwary people below it. And that dark, hollow space inside the Grandfather clock is not the start of a bottomless passage to Australia. Bill also had great fun on the beautiful coastline of South Africa's Kwazulu Natal with things like puffer fish, or 'blaashoppies'.

When startled, these fish fill with water and swell up, thus appearing larger and more frightening to a predator. If you startle them really badly, Bill told us, they would ingest too much water and explode. I wonder if anyone has actually catalogued evidence of such idiocy in a puffer fish? Then there was the brackish tea-coloured, dark and silent lagoon at Uvongo Beach, where apparently an extremely large Groupa (Rock Cod) resides. This evil fish has been known to suck unwary skin divers out of their wet suits.

The soils in the Fort Victoria region were mostly dense red clay soils, great for pottery, but hard on clothes. Despite Kiwa's singsong voice and game attempts with elbow grease, Sunlight soap and a washboard, those red mud stains are forever.

Each beauty spot was revisited on school holidays, every 'gomo' climbed, 'bundu bashing' through the 'shuteen' (or 'gwandashas') was hot and thirsty work and so dams and reservoirs were for swimming (not irrigation), but the bliss of collapsing from heat exhaustion into the murky depths of green gunge and water scorpions made it all worthwhile. Waterweeds smell rotten and, as always, we had to clean up before entering the dining room for a meal.

Also, hosepipes were for drinking out of and not watering the garden—it was just that you had to ensure that your sibling was nowhere near the tap end when you took that drink or the result could be near death by drowning. We fished in the weirs Grandpa had made to store precious water; using home-made bamboo rods with fishing line and bent pins and the endless supply of fishing worms we found in the garden. Well do I remember sitting and dreaming in the cool green shade amidst lushly growing maidenhair fern while the fish nibbled my bait clean off the hook.

For these latter adventures, Gran would fill clean empty jam jars with coffee, tea, milk and sugar and put them into a basket, together with homemade buttery shortbread smothered with sugar. These were enjoyed as an afternoon packed picnic tea caper in one of these beauty spots and we were always happy to oblige, returning to the farmhouse dirty and exhausted.

We ate our fill of farm-grown beef, chicken, pork, dairy, fruit and vegetables. Huge joints of beef were washed down with a single helping of fine red claret. Kiwa cooked the main meals and they were served by the round-faced, shiny James in his crisp white uniform and immaculate cummerbund.

Gran herself was an excellent cook and many afternoons we enjoyed the warm and rich plummy fragrances of Yet Another Pudding escaping from the kitchen, leaving us with happy anticipation of the meal to come. Gran made a new pudding every day so sometimes there was an accumulation, necessitating several helpings of puddings all liberally adorned with rich yellow jersey cream too thick to pour from a jug.

No one will ever forget the day the boys; Bill and Gary, insisted that us girls, Melan, Patty and myself, fetch oranges from the orchard for them to eat whilst they lounged on the wooden fence surrounding the cattle paddocks. We didn't know anything about being sexist in those days; it was simply the natural order of things, so I swear it was without malice that we collected the biggest oranges we could find for their enjoyment. Things turned somewhat sour, quite literally, when teeth were sunk straight into Seville oranges! We learned that these inedible offerings are grown for the sole purpose of turning into marmalade. Needless to say, we were never sent to the orchard on an errand again.

The Christmas holidays were always the best, with the added excitement of the rellies from South Africa paying a visit. Then there were more youngsters our age, Rex, Clifton, Ina and Martin. They taught us games like 'claylaggies'—attaching lumps of thick clay to a very flexible stick and letting fly at each other. You hoped like crazy to never get hit, because it was extremely painful. And you learned to keep your mouth closed. A fast-flying lump of clay crashing into the mouth usually meant a smeary blue bruise and picking bits of clay from between your teeth for the next three days.

The pungent fragrance of fir tree filled the house and there were huge piles of presents under the Christmas tree, winking Christmas lights vying with the soft green lights from the millions of fireflies that appeared around Christmas time. How they lit up the hot summer nights with a magic all of their own. The dinner table was always dressed up with elaborate silver candleholders decorated with asparagus fern and the exotic scarlet-and-gold flame lily flowers, which we hunted up in the afternoon, and silver bowls of nuts and chocolates.

Then there were the years when those rough, grubby, mud-stained cousins grew into something more deadly—teenagers. Together we explored, not the *gomos* but the heady taste of South African wine—complete with its giddy and nauseating side effects. Dad and Muz placed the blame for this particular Christmas caper on Bill and Clifton since they were a few years older. Grandpa's soothing words to Clifton were, 'Don't worry about it. It'll all blow over in due course.' The great fun we'd had wasn't worth the after effects. Like most people, we learned the hard way that if you want to be stupid and drink too much, you have to be tough enough to withstand the consequences. I didn't touch alcohol again for many years.

We loved playing with the 'picanins'—the labour forces' children. Little Godfrey or 'Goddie' as we called him, was a firm favourite. They made us 'catties' and taught us about bird lime. They knew where a lot of birds were nesting and passed on African bush lore. In turn we taught them English, paid good money for the catties which were carved out of old tractor tyres and sneaked goodies from the house. I don't suppose Melan or I was ever classically 'racist' in the sense of bullying or being nasty to them but we were led to believe that African people were inferior. Not only was that wrong, it was also a foolish mistake, and there would be consequences.

As youngsters, we tended to respect the adult Africans, only occasionally getting into trouble with them usually by being silly. This would always be accompanied by a stony-faced stare and they'd let fly with the words, 'Ah, Ah, Iwe!' A scornfully breathed 'Mampara!' was worse, and let you know you'd gone way too far. It was a stinging epithet which invariably had me smarting for hours although I would never admit it.

Mchoko, one of Grandpa's labourers, could imitate almost any bird or animal and we used to love watching him. Grandpa also listened to his expert opinions on such things as the weather forecast. Mchoko was always more accurate than the Met Office. I really do think Mchoko might have ended up as Grandpa's 'Boss Boy' but for his penchant for getting stuck into a large 'chegubu' of 'Chibuku' beer (African beer brewed from sorghum) over the weekends. We never dared arouse any scorn from Mchoko, but for poor Kiwa and James whose task it was to cook and clean for us things were different. Kiwa, with his lined face and little knots of salt-and-pepper hair could look so forlorn and heartbroken if we let him down, and it caused much amusement, I'm afraid. James merely repaid these youthful exploits by stealing some of my things. Boniface, who was young, tall and handsome did become Grandpa's Boss Boy could write and speak impeccable English. We often spent hours in conversation with him after the work of the day was over. Then he got caught sleeping in the maize fields during work hours and we never saw him again.

We loved to hear the Africans singing in the evenings as the tractors would roll into the farmyard with trailers filled with mealies, cotton or sorghum from the day's harvest. The freshly harvested mealies could be boiled and eaten off the cob. Much of the crop was dried in the fields, then harvested and milled into the fine white powder that the Africans would convert into 'sadza' their staple food which they would eat with lip-smacking relish. The cotton bails went off to market to be converted into clothing. The blazing African sunsets became a fiery backdrop to the layers of brilliant, deeply evocative harmonies as they sang and stirred your blood. Still today, living in a kind of exile of our one-time motherland of Britain, some of the more well-known African songs like 'Shosholoza' still have the power to lash my heart raw and bleeding all over again. Then I know the 'deep heart pain' that many victims of the Slave Trade spoke about years before. Africa, with its poverty and pain, its untamable, savage beauty can play dynamic songs with your heart strings and torment you like no other continent on the face of the earth.

But trouble, like fat cumuli-nimbus clouds was looming on the horizon. Our Prime Minister, Ian Smith declared UDI (Unilateral Declaration of Independence) on 11th November 1965 and from that time onwards, war became a possibility. How we loved John Edmond's 'UDI Song' with its lines, *'You can call us rebels, you can call us rogues . . .'* how the thought of being a rebel or a rogue was so romantic! Especially when we were free to live and rule and play in the endless summer sunshine of childhood dreams and games, turning our noses up and our thumbs down at the rest of the harsh and judgemental uncaring world, but we were foolish and there would be consequences.

Things worsened a few notches, when skirmishes broke out amongst the African people who couldn't believe the upstart pretensions of this minority group of colonialists who thought they could own and run a country not theirs. Initially these were squashed by the Police, but like a creeping death plague, things slowly things got out of hand.

Finally those days ended with the 1970's 'bush' war. 'Terrorists' or 'Freedom Fighters' began infiltrating into Rhodesia first from Zambia and then from Mozambique as well when the Portuguese colonialists started leaving. Our own military forces began mobilizing. Men and women in camouflage kit and sporting their new 'gobbie' haircuts which left a pale line around their tanned faces appeared regularly and military vehicles became a common sight. Amongst them were many friends of ours, including Peter Saint. As a young lad, Peter always insisted on being called 'Quickdraw' whenever a game of Cowboys and Indians was suggested. Somewhere we have a cine film of Peter in a pristine new cowboy outfit, white fringe on his fake black Stetson doing a quick draw but struggling to pull the gun out of its holster. Once he does, he's apparently unsure of what happens next and proceeds, for some inexplicable reason, to peer into the barrel. Years later in our teens we dubbed Peter and his good friend Mike, 'Powder Puff and Petal' for fun. They took it all in good part, but suddenly they were grown men. One joined the S.A.S. and the other Support Unit—both elite units in the Rhodesian military, no longer peering down the barrel of a toy gun but with armed with FN (*Fabrique Nationale*) rifles and pointing at a very real enemy they went off to fight the war.

That priceless treasure of childhood—the sheer joy of living coupled with freedom from anxiety became dangerously eclipsed. The 'Bush War' or the 'Second Chimurenga' had begun.

As the war intensified, towns became safer than farms as terrorists saw isolated farmhouses as soft targets, regularly picking on them. The ownership of the land had become a real issue since the original pioneers had appropriated the best of the arable land for farms and moved the Africans into the Tribal Trust Lands; land that was inferior quality and difficult to work. There had been little or no regard for their wants, needs, rightful ownership and worse, their ancestral burial grounds.

The terrorists also targeted African villages, who were even more vulnerable than the farmers, committing unspeakable atrocities to their own kind; raping, pillaging, cutting off lips and making other villagers eat them. They used fear to instill some kind of loyalty to their cause, thereby making life more difficult for the Rhodesian Security Forces.

On the farms, security fences went up. Brick walls were erected in front of the windows which were lined with black-out curtains. Land Rovers were taken into town to be converted into armour-plated 'O-Jays' and we no longer went anywhere barefoot or alone. We always carried weapons, but not the .22 or .410. There were FN's and Uzis instead. Grandpa took his beautiful double-barrel shotgun to town and had the barrels sawn off halfway down, making it a deadly short-range weapon of war and totally useless for anything else.

A 'Bright Light' was installed in the farmhouse—usually an older soldier or Police Reservist for extra security and therefore boringly out of range of our awkward teenage attempts at flirting. A listening device was installed at the dairy, but the amplified snorty nighttime noises and rumbly ruminant stomachs kept people awake, so it was abandoned. And the accoutrements of war were everywhere, making hideous reminders of devastation and destruction on the once-beautiful landscape.

Gran and Grandpa were attacked in the middle of the night. They woke up to the thunderous, clattering roar of fire from AK-47 rifles, but thankfully the house itself was not hit at all. The 'terrs' (or 'gooks' as we often called them) apparently mistook the biggest barn in the yard for the farmhouse, venting their anger and hatred onto a totally innocent barn full of hay bales and grain silos.

Kiwa, the cook, and his family whose house sided the barn, were treated to a hail of bullets and fiery steel raining down on their corrugated iron roof. Physically unharmed, that night must have taken a terrible toll of their nerves. Melan found and kept the casing from an RPG rocket that was fired into the barn, tearing through 19 roof trusses and burying itself without detonating detonating, in the last one.

Further up the road, Uncle Eric and Aunt Ina were also attacked some months later. In the gathering gloom of twilight, a single terr scaled the telephone pole, cutting the wiring and effectively isolating them. His buddies up the hill fired an RPG rocket towards the house—thankfully their aim was absolutely terrible. The rocket flew straight over the house and landed harmlessly in the lands about a kilometer away before detonating; so far away in fact that Aunt Ina and Uncle Eric initially thought Gran and Grandpa were being attacked again.

Then the hand grenade meant for their bedroom hit the wall built in front of the window and exploded harmlessly on the ground. A day or so later, we could examine aghast the shrapnel marks gouged out of that wall, and give thanks that it was only the wall. One of their outbuildings also took the brunt of the attack, and was set on fire, burning irreplaceable family mementoes.

Both times it happened we were able to breathe a sigh of relief. We were even able to joke sometimes about the ineptitude of the terrs that threw pins and held onto the grenades, for instance. Our friend Mike recounted years later a story about one terr who planted a landmine, hotwiring it four AP mines (Anti-Personnel mines) so if one was triggered, all five would detonate in a fierce explosion. As he was putting the finishing touches to his handiwork, one of his 'shamwari's' came over to talk to him; inadvertently stepping on one of the AP mines . . .

Problem with these callous mines was the total lack of ability to discern who was stepping on these hidden death-traps; civilians, little children, donkey carts, wildlife from dainty buck to buffalo and baboons—all could become victims of these deadly detonations. Mike also related an incident where an elderly African villager got caught in crossfire during a contact and ended up badly injured. Mike was devastated by the careless savagery of war that could injure an innocent man. After the firing ceased, Mike rescued the man and carried him bodily for several kilometers over rough terrain before they came to a clearing where the choppers could land and cassavack him out. Time did not dim Mike's pain and years later that incident still made him cry. I never saw Mike cry any other time. But it was no isolated incident, either.

It was around December 1977/January 1978 that terrs in and around Victoria Falls fired a couple of missiles at civilian aircraft (one was a South African Airways aircraft). These missiles malfunctioned and were later found by Security Forces in the bush where they had crashed back down to earth, without doing their deadly work. Around May that year the matter was brought to the attention of Air Rhodesia management, who promptly did all their calculations and called the pilots in for a long lecture. They had tried to work out at what height the aircraft would be most vulnerable (around 700ft on descent and up to around 1 500ft on take-off). Bearing in mind that these missiles are heat-seeking, any calculations had to take into account any and all heat given off by the aircraft. Whoever did the calculations took into account only the heat given off by the four engine exhausts, and not the heat radiating off the silver underbelly or the white crown of the aircraft. Dad and his cousin John Hood, both Viscount Captains did their own calculations and doubled these figures, reckoning anything under 3 000ft was not safe.

It was a constant worry, and we often heard snippets of conversation regarding missile attack. Our family had four men flying for Air Rhodesia: Dad, John, Bill Wragg and Bill Eckert who was a Flight Engineer on the 720's. Chances were, if an aircraft did get shot down, the crew was likely to include one member of the family. We made wisecracks about the 'law of averages' but it was the grim humour of true words spoken in jest.

Many families lost loved ones, or you knew someone who'd been killed. I met up with an old school friend, Peter Battershill, and we'd made a plan to get together after his next call-up, only he never came back. That was war, but you ached for the families who lost young sons, and I am sure my own parents were suddenly relieved they did not have a son.

And then our turn came on the evening of 3rd September 1978 when summer was heating up, the dusty golden grey haze was building up on the horizon, indicative of the start of the rainy season still a few weeks away and the exotic, heady scent of freesias was everywhere. Dad and Muz had invited the family round for the day for tennis, a 'braaivleis' and swimming. Amongst the assorted rellies were John and his new wife Diana. They were due to leave early because John had to operate the evening 'drinks run' to Kariba and bring back a crowd of hot and happy holiday makers. 'I'm going to be late, Rob. Is it okay if I 'phone Ops and maybe tell them I'm not coming at all?' John joked with Dad, his eyes twinkling. He did 'phone Air Rhodesia Operations to warn them he'd be a little late and to hold the aircraft for him. We waved them off and laughed at that. He was the Captain—they had no choice but to wait!

Later on everyone else left, too. The bright heat of the day faded, giving way to a mellow, golden evening. Although the house was quiet, it was as if the atmosphere was permeated with the lingering pleasure we had in the company of the family we cared about. It happened like that occasionally when we were able to put to one side the horrors of war for a few hours and enjoy ourselves, totally unaware of the tragedy about to unfold.

Then the telephone rang. Air Rhodesia's Operations informed Dad bluntly, 'Robin, I need to tell you that something is very wrong. John's plane is missing.'

'You're joking,' Dad replied, his voice cracking, and the shock and horror in his voice ripped the peaceful atmosphere apart. It would be many months before we'd know peace again.

'I'm telling you first so that you can get to Dianne before I have to phone her and tell her.' They roared off to be with Dianne so that she would not be alone when she received the news.

That night first on the six o'clock news then later on the eight o'clock news, the Newsreader informed us, 'Combined Operations Headquarters has announced that Viscount 'Hunyani' VP-WAS, flown by Captain Hood, disappeared at around ten past five this afternoon shortly after take-off from Kariba airport.'

We learned of John's Mayday call, *'Mayday, Mayday Rhodesia 825 help me. We have lost both starboard engines. We are going in,'* was heard from the stricken aircraft shortly after take-off from Kariba airport and then they went missing.

That left Melan and I to answer thousands of telephone calls flying backwards and forwards throughout the night because the evening news bulletin had simply stated Captain Hood without specifying which Captain Hood; Robin or John.

Having a loved one go missing and not know whether they are alive or dead is extreme agony. 'By now John has probably ordered the bar stocks open and free for everyone,' Dad said later on when they came home and we'd try and joke because humour has a way of bulwarking one against tragedy.

Late Monday afternoon whilst at work the news came; VP-WAS had been found. Although there were survivors, the crew was not amongst them. I left work in a rush and collected Melan, trying to get to John and Dianna's house where the family was gathering before the grief kicked in.

Aunt Ina, John's mother, was in the room clutching tightly onto John's takkies that he'd worn only the day before, rocking and weeping for her son. We heard the terrible sounds our cousin made, like an animal in agony. I sat near the pile of stones and cement where John had been building a braaivleis for sunny summer Sundays knowing he would never finish it. Dad was trying to do all the practical stuff, but he aged 10 ten years overnight. His hands trembled slightly and his voice was unsteady.

Every member of the family was physically together yet so dreadfully alone, each encapsulated in their own world of grief; shocked, distraught and struggling to come to terms with the fierce swiftness of death. I know

I attended the memorial service in Salisbury's great Anglican Cathedral and heard the Reverend da Costa's thunderous 'Deafening Silence', but I have no conscious recollection of it, save the fact that there was no coffin for John and that really bothered me. I kept hoping he'd lost his memory in the crash and wandered off somewhere. After a few painful weeks, I had to concede that he was, in fact, never coming back. And I understood the truly irrevocable nature of death.

I have only one memory of the 'wake' after the memorial service, and that was of Captain Keytor, so completely drunk that he staggered and fell over into the flowerbed, but there was no reflex action whatsoever and therefore no attempt to protect himself. We were too plastered to render any meaningful assistance and merely giggled stupidly in an attempt to make him feel better. He'd been one of the individuals whose job it was to sift through the wreckage. All they found of the two pilots was some teeth—the heat from the explosion had been so intense that everything else was consumed. Because dental records had not been kept up-to-date there was no way of identifying whether they were John's or those of his co-pilot Garth Beaumont.

VP-WAS had indeed been hit by a heat-seeking 9M32 'Strela' missile—more commonly known as 'Sam 7' over the Urungwe Tribal Trust Land near Lake Kariba. Although it isn't possible to track exactly how it happened, as with many such disasters, there is usually a series of contributing factors lining up causing the unthinkable to happen, rather than one single factor.

The late afternoon low-angled sun would have been reflecting with red-hot radiance off the silver-and-white body of the aircraft. This provided a good enough initial heat source for the missile to home in on. Right at the end of its deadly flight, the exhaust from an engine would have become the principal heat source, causing the missile to slew slightly sideways on its trajectory, entering the wheel bay on No 3 starboard engine at an angle. There it detonated, directly underneath No 3 engine itself, shattering and splintering fuel and hydraulic lines and electrical connections, rupturing the inboard fuel tanks causing an immediate and intense fire. There was no way the pilots could ever have operated the fire extinguishers located in the wings and even if they did, with a fire that intense, it would not have done much good.

John executed an emergency descent. In the final messages which came from the pilots, John was controlling the aircraft and issuing instructions to Garth on his right, but they knew that they had a roaring fire in the starboard wing. The second message, '. . . *I can't. They're going like f . . .*' was a response from Garth telling John he could not feather the crippled engines.

John would have known that with a fire of such intensity, he had limited time in which to land the aircraft; possibly as little as 2-3 minutes before it burned through, causing the entire wing to shear away from the aircraft. If that happened, there would be no hope for them at all. At that point, he was probably 7 000-8 000ft above the ground when the missile struck. Given the facts of the meeting earlier that year, he would have thought he was within a safe distance from the ground which in fact, was not true.

Another factor which was against them was that September/October time is the height of the 'haze season' which always built gradually towards the end of the dry, cool months of Almost Summer and ahead of the rainy season that normally came around the end of October. With visibility limited by the hazy mess below him and very little time to count on the aircraft remaining intact, he had to make a very quick decision as to the most reasonable spot in which to land. They were still heading towards Salisbury, so it was just descending rapidly on its given heading. Nobody would be able to tell what the speed of descent was, but with two engines wind milling out of control John would have had to use a lot of left rudder and control input in order to try and keep the aircraft flying straight. The port engines would have been slowed down to help compensate for this terrible drag.

To get where he did and land on that small field the way he did was an outstanding piece of flying in terrifying circumstances. When it touched down, the undercarriage was still up and the pilots were still favouring the right wing. Before the aircraft hit an irrigation ditch in the middle of the field, the 'Donga of Death' it had tipped to a slight angle, and the impact with the donga caused it to cartwheel totally out of control. For the pilots and passengers at the front, it was all over. VP-WAS exploded, strewing burning wreckage, suitcases and passengers over a wide area. One can speculate, though. Had the aircraft been landing absolutely straight on when it hit the donga, instead of at that angle, chances are, the whole thing would have flipped straight over, killing everyone on board.

You might say then, that thanks to the flying skills of John and Garth, eighteen of the fifty-six passengers survived the crash. All of them came from the tail section. Some of the more able-bodied, the cries of the wounded and dying in their ears, the sight of carnage, burning bits of broken wreckage in their eyes and the smell of the charred remains of a once-proud aircraft in their nostrils, recovered sufficiently to search for both water and help. The local African people were either too frightened or too hostile to render much help. The injured and dying were left by the aircraft and then the Zipra forces who'd shot the aircraft down, closed in on the wreckage. In the vilest act of war possible, they gunned down those survivors and bayoneted their bodies. The frightened able-bodied survivors had to flee or hide all night long whilst the Zipra forces tried to track them down and kill them also.

A few days later, we watched, grief-stricken and angry, Joshua Nkomo on the national T.V. admitting that his Zipra forces were responsible for the gunning down of an innocent civilian aircraft and laughing with the heady victory of it. Never before and never since have I felt such terrible burning but completely helpless hatred for anyone. It was made only marginally worse when we found out that our Prime Minister; Ian Smith had had secret talks with him, whatever the reason. Possibly he wanted an alliance with the Matabeles that would secure the defeat of Mugabe and the more powerful Zipra forces, who knows?

Those killed in the crash died once, the injured survivors gunned down and bayonetted later died twice, and those left to mourn relived their last moments a thousand, thousand times before we came to anything that resembled closure.

A few weeks later we attended an awards ceremony for John. He was posthumously awarded the Pat Judson trophy for outstanding flying in tough circumstances—a tribute he richly deserved. We, his bereft family, were inordinately proud of him that day and always will be.

Then came the 'in between' period as we would come to call it in later years. Jack Cocking, a very senior engineer with Air Rhodesia had, within a week to ten days, a design for exhaust pipes to be fitted to the Viscounts. Every day, the Air Rhodesia pilots could look across the runway to the military Air Force base, and see their Dakotas taking off and landing with long detachable pipes fitted to the exhausts, the idea being that if the missiles locked onto a detachable pipe, the whole thing would fall away and detonate harmlessly without losing the aircraft or any of the precious lives aboard. Management, in their 'wisdom' decided not to go for it.

These pipes would cause about a 10% loss of performance. They would also mean carrying less passengers and more fuel. There was also talk of painting the Viscounts with a dull green non-reflective paint that would prevent heat reflection, making it harder for the heat-seeking missiles to hit. Management was also very reluctant to use this non-reflective paint, but they did go for a compromise, painting the silver underbelly of the Viscounts, but leaving the white crown intact—which was still reflective and still generating heat.

The pilots were then told they had to fly at low-level when approaching any dangerous zone. This meant that some flights, like the one from Wankie to Victoria Falls was low-level all the way, and could be quite rough and bumpy at times. Then Air Rhodesia were given more information about missiles from the Israeli Air Force, mainly about spiral climbs and descents, which would make following their trajectories very difficult for any missiles. Kariba would remain the most dangerous place of all because of the rough terrain and the huge Urungwe Tribal Trust Land which bounded it. In December 1978 the Airline's management came out with procedures for departures from Kariba to go off at a random heading for ten nautical miles and then climb steeply.

There are hills all around the Kariba basin, any one or all could be harbouring terrs. So Dad and other like-minded pilots still not believing the technical data was accurate, refused to follow these orders. Instead, they took off, flying directly over the lake itself and getting a good altitude before setting course for Salisbury. But some pilots followed the 'random heading' orders because they simply wanted to get to Salisbury, or because they simply did as they were told. They were just following orders.

Dad thought this was ridiculous strategy because it would not be long before the terrs figured out what they were doing and react accordingly. And so it was that on 5th February 1979, Viscount 'Umniati' was shot down also shortly after take-off from Kariba airport.

Captain Andre du Plessis was flying low-level and fast and then climbed very steeply to get out of firing range. But this time, the Strela missile fired at him would not have needed any secondary source of heat from the skin of the aircraft. It just followed the heat from the exhaust, going straight up the tail pipe, detonating and causing instant disintegration of No 2 engine and a total seizure of all the works. The propeller blades snapped off, slicing through the side of the aircraft, cutting the manual controls running to the tail and stalling the aircraft which fell out of the sky in a flat stall. The wreckage was found in a single heap of tangled, twisted, burning remains of machine and people, bearing this out. The pilots got a Mayday out, but they were utterly helpless to do a single thing about their dire predicament. A Police Reserve aircraft at Kariba Airport was dispatched immediately in response to the distress call. There was another Viscount awaiting departure to Salisbury Airport with Captain Tony Weeks at the controls. They made it safely back.

These two tragedies were a turning point in the bush war. Up until that time it had been a kind of civilized war. But the deliberate destruction of civilian aircraft and passengers caused soldiers everywhere to go berserk. Perhaps, much like myself, they were feeling the same gut-wrenching hatred for the unnecessary and unjustifiable slaughter of civilians, who were neither armed nor dangerous. The remaining years of the war became intense and deadly.

I shall always be thankful for my parents' penchant for organizing family days of tennis, braaing and swimming. John and Dianne had been married just three months to the day. We will always have the special memory of that last day to cherish.

After that, things changed radically at Air Rhodesia. Production on the exhaust pipes started immediately. The Air Force lent Air Rhodesia a Strela missile so that they could do tests over the runway at Salisbury Airport. That was when they discovered that everything they knew—or thought they knew—about Strela missiles was not accurate. After everything was done, only then the aircraft were safe from 3 000ft upwards, so take-offs and landings were now performed with the tight spiral formations.

A third aircraft was fired at, but the Strela ran out of oomph, and exploded a short distance from the aircraft, damaging the control tabs on the tail, causing the aircraft to 'jump' in the air. The damage was only discovered later when the pilots reported that the aircraft had been 'difficult to control' and the engineers, checking it over, found the evidence. That is the closest you could ever to get to a Strela missile without becoming its victim.

I remember, too, the evening when one Sven Steiner, who was then a world-leading expert on Strela missiles came to visit Rhodesia and spent the evening having dinner at our family home. It is the only time in our lives we have been able to say we entertained someone of high-ranking status, even if he was not actually a celebrity.

There is also some speculation, although it cannot be confirmed by any one of us that BALPA (British Airline Pilots Association) sent a delegation to Moscow which did more good than people may have thought, because from that time on the Russian-fuelled Zipra terrorists stopped shooting missiles at civilian aircraft when they could have carried on. It might also explain why they never shot down civilian aircraft later on in South Africa. So perhaps the 'Defeaning Silence' was not as complete as we thought it was—it was just that the right things, said at the right time, produced the desired result. But if it really did happen at all, it was highly confidential and as such, remains within a blanket of silence. I must add here, just for the record that it was only Joshua Nkomo's Zipra Russian-trained terrs that shot at civilian aircraft. Mugabe's China-trained Zanla terrs, to the best of anybody's knowledge, did not.

But we were all taking strain with the daily struggles of trying to run a country at war. At school, there were incidents like Suzanne Dobson bursting into our Sixth Form study room in traumatized sobs with the words, 'My cousins hit a land mine last night'—the young Shirley Wickstead who lost both her legs in the blast, and became a war hero. Then there was the day a Police car came to collect Stephanie Dewar and she was sobbing uncontrollably before they were even able to inform her which of her three brothers—all of whom were fighting—had died (later we found out it was Bernard, the youngest).

One of our school friends, Debbie Andrews, got shot in the head in an ambush outside Kariba. Technically brain dead, they kept her alive until they reached Salisbury. I'll never forget having an eye-to-eye confrontation with Debbie over some tall and handsome 'grawb' and then making friends with her all the same because she was a kind and gentle person whereas grawbs will naturally remain that way until they grow up or call-up knocks the grawb out of them. For me, that made her death all the more poignant. Melan's closest friend, Fiona lost her fighter pilot father, Ian Donaldson, when his aircraft exploded in Mozambiquan air space, hit by a ground-to-air missile.

Guerilla-type warfare was very wearing. Gathering around the TV for the eight o'clock news waiting for any communiqué from Combined Operations Headquarters with its bare-faced harsh realities of war, its unsung heroes, its carnage and horror also grew increasingly heartbreaking from Steffi Young, one of the first soldiers to die, right down to the last ones years later. Steffi was hit in the abdomen by an RPG and lived for an incredible two weeks with horrendous injuries, which everyone knew he could not possibly recover from. I was at college with his young cousin, Irene who taught me how to swear in Greek.

We did our best, sending notes to 'Forces Requests' every week for some friend who was fighting, and keeping each others' spirits up, making up goodie parcels for any 'troopie' and knitting balaclavas—all the things women at home did for soldiers on the borders. But a lot of the time, we were out of it. They were forbidden to share information with civilians, and most of the fighting forces had a deep-seated need to talk and drink about the horrors of war that had become their lives, until they found some peace even if it was in the midst of temporary alcohol-induced oblivion.

One weekend Mike took a bunch of us on a camping trip to the Police camping site at Lake McIlwaine. Whilst the guys finished off putting up the tent and sorting out the braaivleis, Melan, Debbie and I got carried away at the thought of silent and unseen O.P.'s (Observation Posts) on the mica-strewn gomo's overlooking the bright waters of the lake. We started posing for them, just to lighten up their afternoon's vigil until Mike, with tolerant humour remarked, 'You girls do realize, don't you, that if there are any O.P.'s up there, they'll all be black!'

Early the next morning, drinking hot coffee, watching a scarlet and gold sunrise over the lake the companionable silence was shattered by a rapid, staccato crackling.

'Sounds like someone's trying to start a badly-tuned VW Beetle,' said Debbie. Suddenly there was a deep, sonorous boom.

'Either it's blown itself up or that's a contact in progress,' laughed Melan.

'That was a mortar,' said Mike suddenly terribly serious and my mouth went dry. Why does fear always make your mouth dry? Mike gauged that it was far enough away not to be an immediate threat. So even here, close to the city in idyllic surrounds, the war wasn't far away.

But people were getting tired. The slogan, 'the people want peace: that is what the people want' kept appearing in songs, adverts, on the radio and TV and got quoted in the nightclubs and bars. Maybe it was propaganda. Maybe it was just the sad reality of a war we could never win.

Fear was an insidious spectral companion kept a constant vigil at your side but you became so used to its presence that it seemed normal. Only when the war ended did you realize just how abnormal it actually was.

And we waited for the war to end so that 'those days' could return—but they never did. They never do. The war ended but life just never, ever returned to what it once was.

We had lost, and it took time for the sickening realization to sink in. The unseen camaraderie that built up when life was threatened and therefore made all the more precious by the sudden, ghastly losses, disappeared virtually overnight and in the wake of its departure, we suddenly grew up. Childhood things were left behind. Christmas at the farm was subdued. Sometimes, it does not matter who is there. It's the people who are not, and who never will be again, they are the ones whose absence makes the most impact. John's loss was so severe that subsequent family Christmases would remain that way.

Eventually a new generation of children would be born and liven up the celebration once again. In the meantime, Patty and Gary cultivated new interests, and moved away from their love of the farm, seldom visiting it. Rex and Clifton finished school and joined the South African army to do their call-up, so their holidays came to an end. We wrote to them regularly—tickled pink by the thought of our handsome, burly cousins having to do a lot of press-ups before the officers would give them any mail obviously penned by a woman. Ina contracted St Vitas' dance and was ill for a long time. Martin was given a part in a movie entitled 'Shangani Patrol' about our ancestors. We spent the entire movie not watching the extraordinary courage of Allan Wilson, but looking instead for glimpses of Martin.

Our grandparents grew old. Shortly after Independence was declared, they sold the farm and moved to the city, mainly because those farms were like an island in a sea of tribal trust land and more farmers were shot and killed in that first year of Independence than had been during the entire war. These farmers who'd either formed 'sticks' to patrol the farms at night, or who had fought and killed terrorists in the war, were still being targeted and terrorists-turned-dissidents could neither forgive nor forget.

They had only been in their new home in Harare for a few months when Grandpa passed away six weeks before their 50th wedding anniversary. That added another family loss as well as the one place in the world that I loved the most was no longer mine to roam freely. Despite the torrid memories of the war and the terrible nightmares, the loss of Rippling Waters remained a stabbing wound. I grieved its passing like an old friend one could visit from time to time, knowing the welcome will always be warm and sincere, a delight, just like the sweet, spicy fragrance of ginger pudding wafting through from the kitchen and simply pick up the pieces where you both left off, because no reintroduction is necessary; just a joyous reunion of good things.

But life has a habit of moving on and bringing other good gifts, as though reaching out by way of compensation. The days of flirtations and 'playing the field' came to a close when an old school friend, Fred Johnson re-entered my life. He was tall, dark and gorgeous—somewhere between Burt Reynolds and Tom Sellick—but he had something neither of them had, to me anyway. He was real; a larger-than-life character. Having come through several years of fighting a war and having death as a constant companion, Fred quickly got round to the extremely important business of packing as much of life as possible into everyday living. He signed up to an apprenticeship with a printing company, sorted out a 'mess' with his friends and hounded me so relentlessly, I ended up inadvertently two-timing some unfortunate bloke who was just around at the wrong time. Fred's quick sense of humour and questionable but hilarious talents with guitar and song livened up many an occasion.

The relationship turned serious very quickly as is often the case in the aftermath of war when people are still very focused on life and death issues. Fred had fought in the Rhodesia Light Infantry during the war and had been one of the stick of soldiers who found John's crashed aircraft where it lay, a smouldering wreck with the bodies of those killed in the crash and the others shot dead by terrorists. As I write this, I have a copy of a photograph of Fred, a soldier, looking through the wreckage of VP-WAS.

Heaven knows what it must have felt like, smelled like, looked like, but Fred never spoke of it; a hangover from the days of war when it was forbidden to talk casually about acts of war. That photograph of Fred had appeared on the front page of the national newspaper some days after the crash.

At last in January 1980, I was able to join the airline myself, now that the immediate danger of war was over, and fulfill a long-cherished dream of becoming an Air Hostess. The first few months the aircraft were still painted dull green wartime colours and take-offs and landings were still executed in the same tight 'corkscrew' formation all of which was supposed to be the safest way of deflecting any heat-seeking missiles that might still be on the prowl. The airline expanded rapidly from regional and domestic routes to overseas, and with great excitement the newly named Air Zimbabwe hired a Boeing 707 from South African Airways. It was painted the new sharp two-tone blue that was Air Zimbabwe's signature colours, with its cheery red and streamlined 'Twiggy Bird' emblazoned on the tail plane and we began an overseas route to England, landing in Gatwick.

As the number of routes expanded, so did the number of aircrews. When I joined there were 33 Air Hostess and when I left there were something like 180—mostly African girls, all of whom we had to train. So there was some irony in the fact that the losing side had to train the winning side.

Three African men were chosen as training pilots, so the flight deck crew had their work cut out for them even more than we did. One of these new recruits also coined a new phrase for flying I.F.R. which usually means Instrument Flight Rules. One morning, on the usual 'breakfast run' to Bulawayo, the white Captain had chosen to operate the 'leg' to Bulawayo, but on the return journey he handed over the controls to the nervous new African First Officer. This young man took off well enough then, once they'd ascended to their designated flight path, seemed to begin aimlessly wandering all over the sky.

'What are you doing?' asked the Captain.

'I'm looking for the road back to Harare,' he replied.

'What!!'

'So I can follow it back . . .' So IFR became known as 'I Follow Roads'—not the best way to fly. But we did find out later that he had been training to become a lawyer, and had been informed by some high-ranking government official that he would become a pilot.

There was always an impassable divide between the aircrews and management. We were, after all, the 'windows to the airline' so everything we did had to be absolutely exemplary. And they gave us a hard time if it was not. The advertising boffins tried to coin the slogan; 'I Fly the Smiling Line' to which we added our own: 'You're lucky. I work for the sods!'

Air crews could be great sports, especially on an aircraft loaded with excitable holiday makers. Sometime during the flight one or other of the pilots would come over the P.A. system and liven up the journey by greeting the passengers and filling them with technical details of the flight and any cricket scores to hand. Occasionally, they livened it up inadvertently, like the time Captain Griffiths forgot to turn the P.A. off. His husky tones complete with red-blooded sigh, floated through the cabin, 'What I'd really like now is some hot coffee and a warm woman!' The 'cabin' hostie shot up to the flight deck to tell him his mistake, but some wag of a passenger put out a hand and stopped her.

'Excuse me, miss, but you've forgotten the coffee!'

Dad's favourite memory was one long haul flight when a drunken passenger seemingly changed his mind about his destination. 'Please ask the Captain to put down the Air Stairs,' he informed the startled Air Hostess. 'I want to get off the aircraft.' Just as well it is a physical impossibility to open aircraft doors at 37 000 feet. One dreads to think what might have otherwise happened that night.

Most passengers were great. Frequently flying businessmen knew the ropes well and fitted in with the system. Holiday makers were simply excited, young and handsome men always enjoyed exchanging some witty repartee with the Air Hostesses. But people with too much alcohol inside them were sometimes dangerous and you always got the odd one who was just plain sucky. One such ill-advised passenger gave me a very hard time, refusing to follow simple Airline safety rules and focusing dead ahead so that I could not get his attention. Irate, I left him to it and went up to the flight deck where the Captain in charge, resplendent in the four Gold Bars of Seniority also happened to be my father and complained to *him*. I know where my limits are concerning my father and I figured this was one occasion I could rely on him to make a difference.

Now on the rare occasion that the Captain appears in the cabin his presence *does* command attention because he is the Ultimate Authority, even that of Mr Sucky Person, who didn't care about the hostess in the two-toned blue uniform, but who didn't sport the gold bars of authority. However, when the man who did, walked down the aisle towards him, leaned over his seat, looked him in the eye and told him tartly, 'If you do not comply with the Air Hostess' request, I will divert this aircraft to Lusaka and drop you off' really did get his attention, as well as those of his fellow passengers who watched the scene with interest. As we were on the way to London, he was risking one heck of a long walk. I'd like to say I didn't hear another squeak from him the entire journey, but I did. After that he became jovial, affable and actually quite friendly.

We also had to get used to the name changes. Rhodesia became Zimbabwe. We no longer lived in 'Salisbury' but in 'Harare' amongst others. Jameson

Avenue, with its long rows of misty-mauve Jacarandas and its ancient 'hanging tree' became Samora Machel Avenue, or more affectionately, 'Sam's Drag' as we called it. Later on, the Presidential cavalcade with its loud and gaudy screen of out runners, black Mercedes and other accoutrements of the new Mugabe regime would go screaming down its length at regular intervals, sirens blaring and become known as 'Bob Mugabe and the Wailers'.

Meanwhile Debbie, Orry, Fred and I made a great foursome and often went places together. It worked well because Debbie was a great friend I'd known for years and Orry was living in Fred's mess. We'd visit them there for swimming parties and saunas, rock music and fun. When it was time for us to go, they'd sit outside the house on the low brick wall and croon 'Babe I'm leaving . . .' and looking so forlorn that Debbie and I would giggle all the way back home.

Air Zimbabwe arrived in England in the heat and the bosky lush greenery of a sizzling June and a whole new world opened up for us, dizzy with delights. Life was beginning to feel good, but six months into peacetime, life held another unexpected tragedy whilst on my second trip to the U.K., and like the loss of John, the tragedy broke up my life and reformed it in a way that I never again returned to the person I had been before.

As the relationship with Fred headed towards serious, there was a break-up of sorts as is so often the case, when one or other partner has to ask the question: 'just how important am I to you?' And whether the relationship resumes or ends depends on how you handle that all-important question. During the break Fred swapped his little red Mini for a motorbike. It was a decision I was decidedly uneasy about, and when we made up again a short time later, I had it in mind to get rid of that bike as soon as was possible.

'Promise me you won't drink and ride that bike whilst I'm away,' I asked Fred as we had lunch at da Guido's Italian restaurant. It was a wintry day in June and I was due to fly out to the U.K. that night for the next six days. Having to leave for a week seemed incredibly long and I just wanted one promise.

'I promise not to ride the bike and drink,' Fred replied solemnly—a promise he broke the very next day. Although he was wearing a crash helmet, he did not tie the chin strap and when he collided with a car, the helmet which would have protected his head came off. He was rushed to hospital with severe head injuries and hooked up to a life support system. Every day he lived through, family and friends dared to begin hoping for a miracle.

After four days, however, the neurosurgeon informed the family that Fred was brain dead. Any hope for recovery was minimal. Even if he did miraculously survive he would be irrevocably changed—the person we all knew and loved had already gone forever, like a beautiful msasa tree fresh in the newness of its russet and gold springtime colours that gets cut down. Without that life-sustaining sap the leaves wilt, wither and finally curl up in a desperate attempt to preserve what's left of their life-force. But their luster, their beauty, the life-force that makes them magnificent and unique, is gone.

The decision to turn the life-support machines off was made. Fred lived for an incredible ten hours, and each hour he lived through, they could watch, hold his hand, pray and still hope. Late in the evening, he finally gave up.

Meanwhile six thousand miles away, I knew something was seriously wrong. I could not relax, eat, sleep or enjoy the hot summer sunshine outside the hotel window. I wanted to phone Fred to make sure he was alright and it was nothing but my own pointless fear, but I was desperately afraid of what I might be told if I did. I tried to imagine how putting Orry on the spot might feel if he was forced to say something like, 'Fred's okay, he's just not home at the moment . . .'

Dad had informed the incoming crew what had happened, but also asked Bob Hill, the Captain, to ensure that nobody told me. He wanted me to be able to get home okay before hearing the news. When we met up with the incoming crew I looked into Bob's eyes and saw the look of deep sympathy that he could not quite hide and my heart slid in my chest.

I returned home the following cold but clear and sunny Friday morning and as I left the aircraft, I saw both Dad and Muz waiting for me on the balcony. That seemed strange in itself because only one parent was required.

When we got to the car, Muz got in the back with me. That was all wrong. Then she produced a flask of coffee and two buff-coloured tablets and ordered me to take them. I found out later that they were Valium. She never gave me tablets, not even painkillers after a bicycle accident left me bruised and grazed. My world fell apart. 'What's all this?' asked a voice quite unlike my own. I looked at the words, trying to figure out what they said.

'Fred has gone to join John and Grandpa,' another unfamiliar voice said, although it came from my mother's lips. That same dreadful icy feeling that my heart was being torn loose from its moorings; that awful gut-wrenching cry, *Nooo!* Jesus, please don't do this to me, not again, not *now*. He was so young, so *alive*. But there was no comfort, only harsh reality and there was enough time for me to go home where kindly hands helped me get ready for his funeral service.

I remembered those last few days when, instead of the outgoing fun-loving larger-than-life character he was, he had become something else instead. He had a quietness and contentedness I'd never seen before. In time, I wondered if he had known that he was going to die—a feeling that Charmaine had also had. We all have our fears and Fred would never have wanted to be what he called an 'oxygen thief'—a person unable to give back to society. Life after the accident would have been intolerable to him.

The only livable part of each day was the first few seconds after waking, before the memories crowded in. I asked myself the same question that countless other grief-stricken people have asked down through the ages: 'Why is the sun still shining? How can that darn radio announcer sound so cheerful? Don't they know what's happened . . . ?'

How often Fred had sung that old Sunday school favourite, 'so let the sun shine in, face it with a grin . . .' it would be many months before I would smile again. Death always raises the question of where the loved one might have gone. And the memory of that cheerily-sung chorus gives me some hope that Fred is once again whole, alive, safe and resting in the everlasting arms of God the Father.

I could never escape the memory of that awful trip when somehow the unseen realm was made known to me—knowledge that I could not possibly have had in the natural and yet I knew what had happened to Fred all the same. But it would be many months before anyone finally plucked up enough courage to give me the raw details because the accident had been his fault. It was at the hands of my friend Debbie that I finally found out the truth, but Debbie's hands were kind, strong and very sensitive. Yet I could not escape the fact that I was partly responsible for his having had a motorbike at all. The guilt was almost unbearable. One day I plucked up the courage to speak to Charmaine, Fred's sister and Rod his closest friend about the guilt I felt. Charmaine reassured me that I was not to blame in any way. Fred had made the decision himself.

Grief cast a pall over subsequent trips to the U.K. and finally I gave up my dream of Air Hostessing, realizing that there was no way I could ever come to terms with the loss that had been inextricably interlinked with it until I did. By that time the sharply smart two-toned blue had been ditched in favour of the earthy colours of Africa: green, yellow, red and black and the cheery-red and streamlined Twiggy Bird replaced with a yellow chicken closely resembling a pregnant brick and therefore not something one would immediately associate with flying.

Much of the subsequent years were shaped by these two tragedies: one an act of war resulting in an ordinary civilian becoming a war hero. On many family occasions a toast was said in John's memory and honour. If you type any of the key words, VP-WAS, Viscount 'Hunyani', Captain John Hood or 'The Deafening Silence' into your search engine, you will find around 300 websites dealing with the tragedy, and on some of them you will also see the photograph of Fred taken that awful day. As I write this, Keith Nel's book, 'Viscount Down' is in its final stages of publication. The other also a hero of war, a man willing to dedicate his young life to serving his country and who survived the whole war only to die a tragically and needlessly—a terrible lesson to learn for the rest of us youngsters that the world after war did not necessarily exclude death and those mistakes we all make one time or another could cost life. But nothing has been taught until something has been learned. Since that time many, many more people have died in the same way, and one wonders when the lesson will finally sink in.

Even after the war ended, death was still an inescapable fact of life. Years later this is still true of the country—one way or another. And yet, when I look back now over the lives and loss of people like John and Fred, I wonder if they themselves wouldn't perhaps prefer us to learn lessons of *life* from them, and remember them in life as they truly were, no matter how short their lives. John would rather we remembered one of his endless quips than his final plea, 'Mayday, Mayday, Rhodesia 825, help me . . .' Fred, fizzy with youthful expectancy and gilded by afternoon sunshine, would rather hear us sing, 'So let the sun shine in . . .' with gusto and remember the hilarious capers he invented for Dr Suess' 'Tweetle Beetles' than K C and the Sunshine Band's painful pleading 'Please Don't Go'.

At this time God, in His infinite wisdom and mercy, taught me about another war, a heavenly battle that will rage until time as we know it ceases to exist. It will also contain persecution and betrayal, especially for those called into leadership positions. One could almost say that these things are prerequisites for good leadership. As in all wars, we are not guaranteed to come out of this one alive either. Our amazing leader, Jesus Christ suffered all these things too, and He may call upon us to go through the same experiences as He Himself once did. The big difference, however, is that it is one we cannot fail to win because this war has already been won and we are privileged to be called upon to play a part in the end time skirmishes.

POTHOLES BELOW THE SURFACE THOUGHTS

LOOKING TO JESUS, THE AUTHOR AND PERFECTER OF OUR FAITH

The bible is split into two separate covenants: the Old Testament covenant of the Law, which was given through Moses and the New Testament covenant of Grace, which came in the person of Jesus Christ. The difficulty we sometimes have reading the bible is trying to work out where the righteous requirements of the Law fit in with this amazing and free gift of grace. To make matters more complex, whilst Jesus Christ was still on earth, He was still under the Law. It was only after His death, resurrection and ascension that the new covenant of grace was established. So when we study His words we have to bear in mind that He often pointed to the Law. He did that not because He wanted us to keep the Law but to show us that although the Law is—and always will be—God's perfect standard, but trying to keep it is absolutely impossible. That's why He gave us His grace. We can preach Law or we can preach grace, but it is my understanding that the biggest problem comes when we mix the two covenants because then we end up negating them both. This is the issue the Apostle Paul deals with in the book of Galatians. However, unless we preach FULL-ON grace, peoples' lives will not undergo a full-on transformation.

When I came across the verse from Revelation 13: 8 that stated: '. . . the Book of Life of the Lamb, slain from the foundation of the world' and again from 1 Peter 1: 18-20 which states: '. . . knowing that you were not redeemed with corruptible things like silver or gold, from your aimless conduct received by the tradition of your fathers, but with the precious blood of Christ, as of a Lamb without blemish or spot. He indeed was foreordained from the foundation of the world, but was manifest in these last times to you . . . .' that my understanding was radically transformed.

In some mysterious, unfathomable act of God, Jesus Christ was slain before the foundation of the world. Not Satan when he began his rampage knew this and not people truly knew about the shed blood of Jesus until He died on the cross centuries later. The deep implication of this truth is that grace has always been with us, underpinning our world and glorifying God in a way that an unfallen world never could have done. Grace has been available to every single one of us before we were ever created. Death and hell were never God's intention for the people He has always loved so much. But way back in the Garden of Eden when something went so horribly wrong, the whole pattern of our existence has changed because of one man's—Adam's—sin.

There were two trees in the Garden. The Tree of Life (Jesus and the gospel of grace) and the Tree of the Knowledge of Good and Evil (the Law), and so when first Eve and then Adam chose to disobey God's one and only rule and eat off the second tree, the whole nature of creation changed. Before that, we would have lived out our allotted life span in close fellowship with God before going to live with Him forever.

Hell was created as a final place for fallen angels, not people. So all through the bible you will find the same theme surfacing time and again. Inclusion into the kingdom of God came before exclusion from it because the Tree of Life is still available to all of us. And as you get to know this wonderful God of ours, you will find that He is not the One who excludes us.

So let's have a brief look at how the Law came into being and why it's not the covenant God would have ever given us had Adam not sinned, had we trusted Him completely the way He always wanted us to.

Exodus relates the story of the Israelites having been stuck in Egypt, the place of slavery, for 400 years. One generation after another had come and gone, praying for release and surcease from the hardship, but nothing had changed except for the worst. Finally the long awaited time had arrived and Israel was able to make their bid for freedom.

In a series of confrontations between Moses, Aaron, Jannes and Jambres in the court of Pharaoh the result was a number of plagues, after each one, Pharaoh hardened his heart and would not allow the Israelites to leave until the final devastating plague during which God instituted the first Passover.

In Exodus chapter 12, God gave Moses very specific instructions for the Passover:—

- Each family was to take a male lamb of the first year without blemish. There was no be enough for the family and nothing was to be left over.
- All the lambs were to be slaughtered at twilight. The blood was to be collected in basins and applied to the doorposts and lintels of the houses using branches of hyssop.
- They had to roast the lamb, eat it in haste together with unleavened bread and bitter herbs, all dressed ready to leave.
- During the night the Lord would pass through the land slaughtering all the firstborn from every household and flock where there was no blood on the doorposts and lintels.
- He would pass over every house where the door was thus adorned with blood.

The Israelites were not automatically protected from this plague because they were Israelites. It was the blood on the doorposts and lintels that saved them from the savage plague of death which struck that night.

In the aftermath of the devastation, the Israelites were finally allowed to leave. But even after they did, they were pursued by the Egyptian army.

The Red Sea parted for the Israelites, but closed in their wake, drowning the entire Egyptian army.

On the heels of this supernatural deliverance, on the banks of freedom, Miriam (who was closer to 90 than she was to 80) picked up her timbrel and led the most massive praise and worship service they'd probably ever had. What a night of colossal celebration that must have been reaching and echoing around the mighty vaults of heaven.

Yet there they were, just three short days into the desert, arriving at Marah, the place of bitter waters and things have changed dramatically. It's so easy to praise and worship God when He's performed a magnificent miracle; how hard it is in the face of adversity.

God did not promise a life of sunshine and happiness, not even for His chosen people. Things go wrong. But everything that happens to us has passed through His sovereign hands and if it hurts us, it has got to have hurt Him also. Much later on Jesus warned, 'In this world, you will have trouble.' And when He did so, He wasn't kidding.

Faith should never focus on the things that are seen, but on that which is unseen. Why? Because what is unseen is eternal! But three days into the murderous heat and burning sands, an all-consuming thirst was becoming a very real threat to their survival. This was no triviality they were lacking. Experts point out that humans can exist without food for far longer than they can without water. Our bodies are made up largely of fluids and most bodily functions require water as part of their processing and three days without water is risking serious health problems.

Whilst things on earth are constantly changing, shape shifting, unreliable and temporal, the things that are unseen and eternal are not. When I am embroiled in some difficult trial, it always helps me to focus on God and remind myself that where He lives there is a place of complete tranquility and peace. His domain is not disturbed by any form of human suffering and it is all perfectly aligned, unbroken, unchanged, unchanging, and totally reliable. Nothing ever occurs to God. He wants us to live in this perfect peace and tranquility too. That's why His word says, 'He will keep you in perfect peace, whose mind is focused on Him.'

God can, and does, often help us through our times of trouble, grief, trauma and sorrow. He can bless us with any or all of the 58 blessings mentioned in scripture, many of which are temporal. But His focus is and always remains on the eternal.

I don't know why so many people honestly and earnestly believe that after committing their lives to God, everything is going to run smoothly from that point on. In fact, the reality is that many people suddenly find it gets worse, gets harder and that can be confusing when values start to change. So it was for the Israelites when they put their trust in God 100% that they found themselves in the place of harsh misery.

God, through the agency of Moses, led them to Marah. The Israelites were there by divine appointment. If we know that God has led us to a point of hardship, we find that this can be one of the hardest tests of faith there is. Why would God lead us to places like Marah? This question often has become a universal one: the why's of undeserved suffering.

After three days in the desert, they were so parched they probably felt they could have drunk anything, except this water. There was something so vile about it that it was impossibly unfit for human consumption, even in their desperate circumstances.

Water in the desert can come from several different sources and some of it is good. But the waters of Marah came up from the earth. The things of the earth always taint the things of the Spirit.

Let's think about the water they left behind—the sweet waters of the Nile. I've read that these waters have an exceptional, unique flavour. Every year the Nile flooded, bringing mineral-rich silt and depositing it along its banks and the crops produced from there were amazing.

One of the things that changes when we become Christians is that we find we now have an enemy. Satan, who probably didn't care a whole lot about us when we were in his territory, now sees us as a potential threat. If he can't stop us from becoming Christians, he will turn to another weapon in his arsenal to prevent us from becoming effective: temptation and accusation. He isn't overly creative; he just keeps using the same old weapons over and over again.

'Look behind you, back over your shoulder and think of all the good things you still had when you were in Egypt,' he seemed to be taunting the Israelites in their weakened state. They conjured up mirages of the sweet water, onions, melons and garlic they had in Egypt. We humans can forget all about the misery very quickly as the enemy presents a rosy picture of life that really is not true. No matter how good food tastes in slavery, it can never, ever compare to simple, humble bread eaten in freedom.

Hardships reveal exactly what's inside us: the grumbling, the anger, whatever it may be. Circumstances cannot make you grumbly. They can only reveal the grumble in you. People cannot make you angry. They can only reveal the anger already there. 'The person who angers you . . . controls you' is worth thinking about—that person has revealed in you something that needs to come under God's submission. That's why peoples' anger does not profit the kingdom of God.

But they were thinking to themselves: if this is what God's freedom is all about, would they rather live as slaves in Egypt than die as free people in the wilderness? They thought they'd merely exchanged one set of terrible hardships for another. Beloved child of God, living the life of plenty in slavery is never the better choice. Rather die a free person by the waters of Marah.

Obviously, Marah is not the Lord's best for us either. He had something infinitely better in mind. Somewhere up ahead of them lay the Promised Land, and one 'flowing with milk and honey.'

Since they were 'murmuring' a lot, it's a word that deserves special attention. This word with its gentle, but unhappy sound is worth a special mention. 'Mur' is what babies do when they're unhappy. The fact that it is repeated, murmur means the Israelites were giving it a double dose of grumbling. The trouble with grumbling and complaining is that it is engendered by a lack of faith that becomes nothing more than a total stumbling block. Their whole vision was taken up with the desert around them, their life-threatening thirst. When we focus more on our own immediate needs rather than on God we may also end up with a tendency to complain. They behaved like children but how God treated them was absolutely amazing. We'll look at it in a moment.

In this case the Israelites did what most of us do when we're faced with a terrible situation—they blamed someone else—Moses. Why would God bring them to this place of disaster? Maybe Moses had got it wrong. And they cried out at him: 'What's the point of coming here? What are we supposed to drink? We're just going to end up dying here in this terrible wilderness.'

Over the course of our lifetime, we all ask God for the things that we think will make us happy. Years ago, when I was counselling, I remember time and again young adults who became so obsessed with the idea of marriage that it became the mainstay of their prayer life.

They got married all right but some of them ended up with disastrous marriages. They thought their single lives were unfulfilled and unhappy. Yet all their marriage ended up doing for some of them was exchange one set of trials for another. Desire for change sometimes only brings worse affliction. Trials sometimes merely shape shift from one form to another. For the Israelites they were desperate for water, but when they found it, they could not drink it. The trial merely shape shifted. Don't be too impatient to exchange one set of trials for another.

Trusting God in the midst of trial is the right thing to do, but in this case only Moses did it. He cried out to God. Three million grumbled and one man prayed. And it was the praying man who was given the answer. If you want guidance to get you through the hard times, then keep your eyes firmly fixed on God and see what He can do.

God showed Moses a tree, and when Moses cast the tree into the waters, they were made sweet. Everyone whooped for joy and splashed right in. It was the same waters, but its properties had changed. I don't think there was any magic ingredient in the tree. Any time you read the scriptures and find the imagery of a tree, it's a good idea to check and see if it will fit in with the cross of Jesus Christ. The old Aramaic words for 'tree' and 'cross' and 'wood' all have the same root.

So here we find a very valuable principle. The application of the cross of Jesus Christ is the only thing that will draw sweetness out of life's bitter experiences. Well, we may not choose adjectives such as 'sweetness' and 'bitterness' to describe life's experiences, but I think you will get the point. Taking those experiences to the foot of the cross and leaving them there means that you can claim the promise that 'all things work together for good for those who love the Lord and who are called according to His purposes' The cross of Jesus Christ can bring out eternal value in any suffering we may go through, and in the light of eternity, we will never see it as pointless and purposeless. Focusing on God first and then looking to the problem puts all things in their right perspective, for then we will have a GREAT God and a light and temporary problem. That doesn't detract from any of the suffering we may go through, by the way. Heartbreak is something that happens in life, sadly, but with the eyes of faith, we can put it in the context of the bigger picture and reassure ourselves that in God's timing, God's best will come out of it.

We are not told specifically what made the waters of Marah bitter. And that's the truth of many of our trials. God chooses never (or very rarely) to inform us of why we had them in the first place. Sometimes they are purely a test of faith and nothing else. Every single Christian will have their faith tested at some time, probably more than once.

This tree could also be a type of 'tree of life' which can also mean that no matter how vile a place is, the tree of life can still grow there! Live your life in this continual expectancy of what God can do. Don't limit His greatness.

In this particular instance, God was testing the Israelites. He showed them their point of need and then He introduced them to one of His characteristics that would meet them at that point of need. 'I am the Lord who heals you,' He said.

Unfortunately, with the English translations, we lose the significance of many of the names given to God in the Old Testament because He is simply called 'God' or 'Lord' but the Israelites had many more names for Him than that and each one denoted a characteristic of God that meets us at a point of need. Here He is revealed as 'Yahweh Rophe'—the Lord who Heals.

If we are never shown that point of need, we will never understand the nature of God who can meet us at that point of need, even in the times of harshest trial.

After Marah came the wonderful place of Elim. This was their second stopping place, and what a magnificent place of peaceful rest it was, with 12 springs of water and 70 palm trees. Elim is a type of refreshing in the power of the Holy Spirit. Later on in the New Testament book of James, Marah becomes linked to the Law hidden like a bitter root in our hearts, whilst Elim reflects the fresh, restful and sweet outpourings of grace. Mixing the two sources together produces the 'lukewarm' flow that is likened to Laodicea, which is fit for neither covenant.

But after Elim, they were once again in the harsh environs of the desert. Have a look at all the chapters of Exodus, from the Passover to the giving of the Law at Mount Sinai and when you do, I hope that you will get the same exciting picture of grace that I got when I read it in the early hours of the morning. God seems to like giving me startling revelations in the early hours of the morning! Then I cannot get back to sleep as whole chains of facts and ideas about Him start slotting into place! DESPITE THEIR MURMURING, WHICH SHOWS DISOBEDIENCE AND LACK OF FAITH, THEY WERE STILL UNDER GRACE! Moses prayed, and God gave them the answers! Wow! He gave them wonderful manna, He gave them water out of the rock and every time they murmured, grumbled complained, His sovereign hand gave them what they needed. From the time of deliverance from Egypt to the time the giving of the Law, there is no record of any Israelites dying. See if you can find the same truth. I sometimes think it is worth looking at things the bible doesn't say, as well as the things it does. That's when the bible shows us great truths rather than simply telling them.

Then came a statement of great tragedy. In Exodus 19: 8 the whole picture changed when they said to God: 'All that the Lord has spoken, we will do.' So in that statement, they were saying to God, 'stop assessing or blessing us based on Your goodness. We are well able to be obedient, so assess us and bless us on our obedience.'

So Moses went up Mount Sinai and received directly from God the tablets of stone containing the Law and from that point onwards, everything changed for the Israelites, because they were no longer under the gracious righteousness of God, but were being judged on their own righteousness. Straight away, God warned Moses to tell them not to go near His mountain or they would be put to death. So that is what happened. The Israelites made a golden calf almost straight away, to prove that our own righteousness is truly awful, and three thousand people died almost immediately afterward. And from then on, every time they grumbled, they died because basically grumbling is a lack of faith that makes a holy God very angry. Idolatry is also always an outworking of being under the Law.

The Law required that sin cost life, and therefore life was required to pay for that sin. Right from the terrible tragedy after Adam and Eve's initial sin where an innocent garden animal was slain by the hand of Almighty God Himself to clothe their painful and fearful nakedness it has been the same. Along with the giving of the Law came a complex sacrificial system was instigated during the time of the building of the Tabernacle of Moses.

Today, the righteous requirements of the Law have not changed. It's still the same as it always was, but it has been fulfilled in Jesus Christ. All of God's anger and wrath against the self-righteous sin of people was taken out on Jesus at Calvary; the ultimate Passover where, if you think about it, God passed over us and struck Jesus instead. In Matthew 5: 17 Jesus said: 'Do not think that I came to destroy the Law or the Prophets. I did not come to destroy but to fulfill.' Thankfully He has fulfilled it, since we are entirely incapable of fulfilling it ourselves. Moreover, since He has fulfilled it, before the foundation of the world, we are totally reassured that inclusion into the Kingdom of God came before exclusion from it. In fact, it is we who exclude ourselves from His Kingdom; it is not God who excludes us.

Before I shut this study down, I just want to ponder on some of the chief differences between the Law and grace:—

- The Law is about **achieving** but grace is about **receiving.**
- The Law is **given;** something that was done in response to human demand. Grace **came** out of free choice and because of deep, abiding love for people.
- The Law points each one of us to **our own efforts** whereas grace points us to the **cross** of Jesus Christ.
- The Law is **impersonal**, all about a set of rules. Grace is about a Person, a **divine Person.**
- The Law can point out where you went wrong, but **it can never make you holy**.
- The grace of Jesus Christ is that **He gives you His grace and that is what makes you holy!** Stop worrying about trying to do things in your own strength.

Grace is free, but it is not cheap. It cost Jesus Christ everything He had, so we do not use this precious gift to go on willfully sinning. We live in the power of the righteousness Jesus has given us—the grace He gives us comes with a corresponding hatred of evil. When God looks upon us, He sees us as covered in the blood of His precious Son. And ultimately God is only interested in asking us one question: *WHAT DID YOU DO WITH MY SON?* It is a positive answer to this question that allows us a place in the Lamb's Book of Life, and nothing else. Whoopah! Enjoy this wonderful gift of grace today and every day!

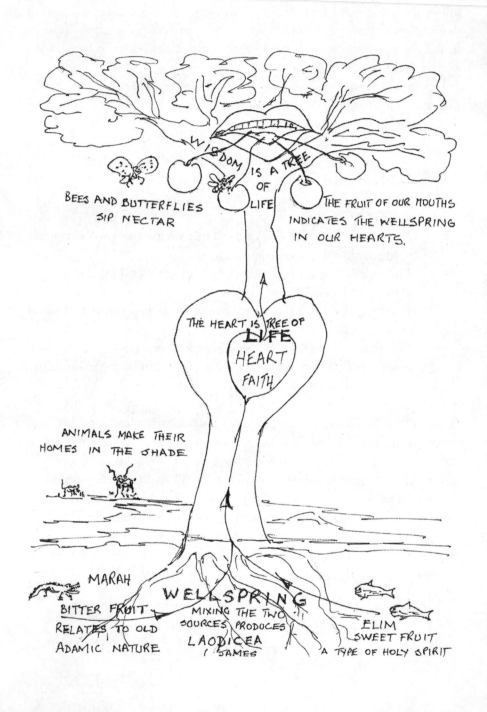

POTHOLES SHORT THOUGHTS

MUDFLATS AND MOONSHINE

'The Church has given us a painting of Kingsbridge Estuary,' Sally said, 'but it's a picture of when the tide is out.' I can't miss the slight note of disappointment in her voice.

Kingsbridge Estuary is beautiful, just decidedly more so when the tide is in. The seabirds and boats bob on the water and bright coruscations of sunlight ripple and refract, giving radiance that fills you with joy. When I look at it, especially on a warm spring morning with new life burgeoning everywhere after the long winter, I have an idea of how my soul will feel on Resurrection Day.

When the tide is out, however, the scene loses much of its charm as the dark greenish-brown of the mudflats appear. It's covered in intermittent blobs of green-gunge seaweed, and if you stand close enough to smell it, the rank saltiness will ensure that you draw back quickly enough.

And yet light can change this picture and transform it into something beautiful for God anyway. Driving home past the estuary one night we saw the moon shining with its splendid silver ethereal radiance, lighting up the familiar scene into something altogether different—and truly lovely.

It reminds me that God is Light, and in Him there is no darkness at all. In His light, anything, any situation, any life can be completely transformed. God is like the sun; He makes His face to shine upon those of us who are Christians, and we shine with His reflected radiance on the world around us. My friend that is His grace that flows in and through us to spread His light and His radiance to the world. If we were still under the Law there is no way Jesus would ever have referred to us as light or given us the amazing ability to spread that light because we simply would not have been capable of such a responsibility.

Just the other day, I was in the Sports Centre overlooking the estuary doing my regular, if crazy run, on the treadmill. The tide was out and under the cold, gray wintry skies, the mudflats were at their most unappealing gloomiest. As I ran, though, the clouds dissipated and the bright morning sun shone down turning the scene into such incredible golden brightness that my soul was strengthened and lifted up with joy at the scene before me. It reminds me of the fact that my God can transform anything, from hostile scenery to broken dreams with the glory of His presence.

MEMORY VERSE
Matthew 5: 14:
Jesus said; 'You are the light of the world. A city that is set on a hill cannot be hidden. Nor do they light a lamp and put it under a basket, but on a lampstand, and it gives light to all who are in the house. Let your light so shine before men that they may see your good works and glorify your Father in heaven.'

AS I RAN HOME, THE LORD SAID, 'GIVE YOURSELF A GOOD
SHAKE
AND LET MY GLORY IN YOU BE SPLASHED OUT
ALL OVER THE PLACE'

So, if you see me running around giving myself a good shake
That's what I'm doing!

POTHOLES SHORT THOUGHTS

THE WORDS OF ETERNAL LIFE

How Jesus could handle the bread! From manna in the desert, to the miracles of bread and fish in His teaching ministry, and from the Passover meal He ate before Gethsemane to the wedding feast at the close of the age. We can look on in disbelief or gasp in awe as we watch what He does or we can go one further and participate in that very precious communion.

In John chapter 6, we can read the miracle of bread and fish multiplied. Of course Jesus can do that—take our smallest offerings and multiply it into something millions of times bigger than we could ever hope or imagine. Look what happened afterwards—loads of people followed Him, and quite naturally too. Couldn't we all do with Someone who could provide the increase, especially when money is very tight?

When they did though, He challenged their motives with a very disturbing sermon. In essence He informed them, 'For My flesh is food indeed, and My blood is drink indeed. He who eats My flesh and drinks My blood abides in Me and I in him . . . He who eats this bread will live forever.'

For anyone, the thought of eating human flesh or drinking human blood is bizarre, but for Jews who had the added dilemma of the Law forbidding such practices, they simply could not accept this concept. From then on, opposition to Jesus began to increase and He would be rejected by the very people He came to save.

Once alone with His disciples, He challenged them asking, 'Do you also want to go away?' Peter answered Him, 'Where would we go, Lord? Only You have the words of eternal life.' Despite being unable to understand, Peter was determined to remain steadfast and loyal.

Eventually this concept would become known as the mystery of the gospel and it didn't mean the literal eating of flesh and drinking of blood. Instead, it meant that Jesus would live in us and we would live in Him. Jesus was totally both human and divine, and we His church, can be the same—human but alive with His divine life. We only have to believe! But watch out for the tests of faith that God will bring into our lives. Like this one, they may be simply bizarre and difficult to understand. Keep pressing into Jesus even when you don't understand. The Righteousness of Jesus Christ lives in you! You rule and reign in righteousness and peace! The rewards will be more than you could dream or imagine.

MEMORY VERSE
John 6: 54
'Whoever eats My flesh and drinks My blood has eternal life, and I will raise him up on the last day.'

GRACE FROM START TO FINISH IS THE WORK OF JESUS CHRIST

GRACE IS GOD AT WORK AND THE WORK IS FINISHED. IT IS ALL DONE!

<u>Potholes Joy bag</u>

<u>ALL CREATURES GREAT AND SMALL</u>

I have two dogs: one an incredibly sweet but very daft Great Dane called Benjie. The other is a tiny Miniature Pinscher (affectionately known as 'Min Pins' by their devoted owners) called Aspen who is cheeky and smart. Quite why I have decided to live with this combination, I do not know. It is totally inexplicable. Only other dog owners with two such diametrically opposed sized canines will understand the difficulties incurred by such lifestyle choices. Therefore, these are the instructions I intend to teach them if at all possible.

TO BENJIE:-

-   I am a Great Dane. I am not a Min Pin. I will not try and climb into my mistress's lap every single time she sits down.
-   I will also try not to sneak up onto her bed at night. This is simply Mission Impossible.
-   I will try not to push Aspen downstairs by my sheer bulk. She also has a right to be here.
-   I will try not to stand on Aspen. This will annihilate her altogether.
-   I will not lick my nether regions then try and lick my mistress's face.

- I will not try and join in when my mistress's boyfriend is trying to tickle her on the couch.
- I know I can reach across the tabletop but this does not mean that any food left thereon is truly meant for me to eat.
- The pooper-scooper is not a toy.
- I must not chase cars and bite bumpers.
- I must not rush up to complete strangers in the park and try to greet them with my big, meaty and happy smile. They do not find this particularly friendly.
- I must not lean on people, particularly elderly people.
- I must not chew on chords that come out of funny-looking holes in the wall.
- The vet is someone who is saving up to buy a new Porsche. I will not contribute to his Porsche fund by eating unnamable gunge in the park and then being sick.
- There is no need to be afraid of the dark.
- Postmen are not burglars.
- Garbage collectors are not stealing things.
- Burglars are not welcome.
- It is more practical to shake rainwater out of coat before entering house.
- Re the above: Humans prefer to remain dry during this procedure.
- 'How sweet!' or 'How cute!' are exclamations which refer to Aspen only.
- I must learn to rely on my size, rather than my intellect, for survival.
- Fire hydrants and chair legs are not the same thing.
- My mistress carries dog biscuits in her pocket all the time. They are not all for me.
- I must not stand straight up suddenly when I'm lying under the coffee table.

TO ASPEN:—

- When my mistress takes me out in the car for a lovely walk on the beach, I will try not to sit in the back window, wearing a devastated expression as though I am being kidnapped.
- I am a Min Pin. I will try not to chase people. This is Benjie's job.
- When my mistress puts me on the lead for a walk I will try not to drag her around the place. This is also Benjie's job. People look ridiculously silly when being dragged around by a very small dog. The same cannot be said for being dragged around by a Great Dane.
- I must not lie on my back and expose my nether regions when my mistress's mother comes to visit. She finds this unacceptably unladylike.
- The pooper-scooper is not a toy.
- I must not take offence and growl when people mistake me for a rat.
- I will not bite people who think I am cute and want to stroke me.
- The next German Shepherd/Border Collie/Retriever/Bulldog that I try to bite might try to bite me back.
- Not all German Shepherds/Border Collies/Retrievers and Bulldogs are afraid of me, just because Benjie is.
- I really should not chase the neighbour's cat. He is bigger than I am. He also has sharper claws.
- Postmen are not burglars.
- I really ought to depend on my intellect, rather than my size, for survival.
- I must not go berserk at a fuel station when my mistress goes inside the shop to pay for the petrol. She will return in due course.
- I do like chasing flies and other bugs, but I really must remember that chasing bees does not have quite the same outcome.
- I can scootch my bottom along the grass but not when the Grandparents are visiting.
- I must not roll toys behind the fridge.

INSTRUCTIONS TO ME FROM MY DOGS:—

- Please make sure we really do understand you. This may mean learning to pronounce your words correctly.
- Please do not attempt to communicate to us in barks, whines or growls. Especially growls. You will find it much simpler if you just use plain English.
- You do the pushing. We'll do the pulling.
- If you push me (Aspen) too hard, I may bite you. Then you may chide me. And call an ambulance.
- If you push me (Benjie) too hard, I may open my mouth and swallow you whole.
- Make sure we're comfortable. Then we'll be happy and so will you.
- Thank you for providing us with such a comfortable bed. Please feel free to order a similar one for yourself.
- When we are asleep and you are the one awake, please do what the burglars do and walk around on tiptoe and speak in whispers. We do not wish to be disturbed.
- On the other hand, if we wake up a lot during the night please administer sleeping tablets. You will find it much easier to sleep this way. Give us one each. You take two.
- Kindly refrain from snoring. This is worse than your barking.
- When choosing wardrobes please understand that we are not out to impress male dogs. We prefer to dress to irritate other female dogs.
- Please ensure you read the newspaper before we tear it up.
- Do explain any mistakes we've made. Dogs prefer persuasion rather than force—any day.
- Sling chairs, side chairs and coffee tables are uncomfortable furniture for dogs to lounge on. A comfortable, padded rocker would be much better. Preferably one for each of us. Do get one for yourself, also.
- We like to see paw prints on your clothes.
- We don't mind if the vet gets a new Porsche.
- The garden needed some renovation anyway.
- We have a mental list of people we would like to spay or neuter.

- If we are getting fat, it is because you are not getting enough exercise.
- Yes, we do like to make a fool of you occasionally. More often than not you do this without any help from us.
- Regardless of how cute/loyal/cuddly we are, do remember that you are still sharing your home with a wolf. Instinct prevails. We do not mind sharing your food with you, but it is better if you do refrain from trying to share ours.

Whilst we are on the subject of your food, do be sensitive about what it is that you share with us. You can eat it happily enough but some of it is toxic to dogs:

Chocolate has some sludgy character called Theo Bromine hidden in its dark and rich, creamy depths. Theo does not like us dogs at all. He'll track us down and may eventually kill us. DON'T give us chocolate. This is not spoiling us with your love, it's murder. The same goes for fresh grapes and dried raisins. Don't ask us why these are toxic. They just are. So are bread dough and alcohol, but it remains an inexplicable mystery to us as to why any human would try and feed us such weird stuff.

And, last of all, when the time comes for us to take that final journey, please do not leave us in the kindly, but stranger hands of the vet. You stay with us, cuddle us and talk to us until it is all over. Then plant a Garden of Remembrance with our favourite trees, flowers and a couple of hydrants . . .

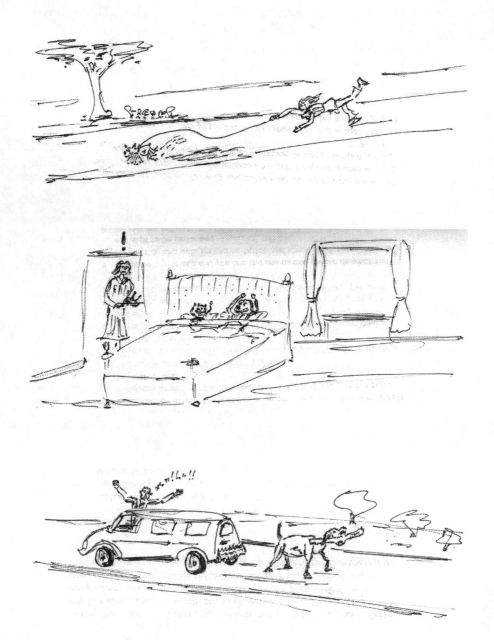

CHAPTER TWO

SURVIVAL COURSE ON THE UMFULI RIVER

The trucks slid to a halt, raising clouds of soft, and white 'plop-plop' dust. I leapt out before it had quite settled, eager to start the adventure of a 'Survival Course' and delighted at the pungent fragrance and wide panorama of Rhodesian bush land, late afternoon sunshine making bright coruscations on the limpid green waters of the Umfuli River.

'Grab your bag,' suggested Melan. 'Gotta set up camp and explore before sundown.' She was the go-getter. I was the dreamer. I looked down at my legs. My suntan had disappeared under a layer of 'plop-plop' dust.

Melan, getting useful straight away, began unloading the trucks, pulling my bag out and dumping it into my hands. For a four day trip into the bush, our bags were pitifully small in keeping with the whole theme of the trip. There were no clean clothes, toiletries or any of the items which usually make life bearable for young teenagers. Only essentials like binoculars, notebooks and pens, a camera, walking boots and a hat had been included on the check list.

Melan and I had been invited to take part in a survival course on the Umfuli River. *Um . . . foolish . . .* and the sort of course relegated to soldiers in training would have been more appropriate; it certainly wasn't for 'sissies'. We weren't on our own, just Special Guests of Dave Rushworth, who'd organised it, alongside a school full of completely unknown entities marauding on our private space. Mount Pleasant High School from North of the Railway Line and that, straight away, branded them as rich, snobby and incapable of correctly handling a bush trip.

The idea was to make out as if we had survived (uninjured) an aircraft crash in the middle of the gwandashas, and had to stay alive until help arrived or more proactively, go and look for help. That meant having just the clothes you were wearing. No hairbrush, no toothbrush, no change of clothes, no deodorant or make-up. Food had to be found, so none of the usual teenage essentials like crisps, chocolates and fizzy drinks. We also had to find out very basic things like which leaves really did make the best toilet paper and which ones never to use. Take it from me—don't *ever* use large, soft-looking furry leaves for toilet paper. You will hate yourself for many hours afterwards.

'Gather round, everyone,' roared Dave, waving his long, freckled arms at the stragglers and those jabbering and still fiddling in the backs of the pickup trucks. He was as at home with recalcitrant teenagers as he was in the bush. As we gathered into an untidy pile around him, he explained, 'I do want to ensure that you do really survive, so I've allowed a few extras.' With a twinkle in his pale blue eyes, he hauled out another couple of kit bags. For a split second, I got all excited thinking he was going to relent of four days hardship after all and begin distributing food and clothing. But out came plastic water bottles (water had to be sourced and purification tablets added), fishing line and bent pins, a pen knife, matches, mosquito repellent and sleeping bags as the one major concession.

The days were dribbly-sweat hot and the scenery was stunning; the autumn sun shone in a hard blue and cloudless sky, sandy beaches and rocky outcrops overlaid with lush trees, some laden with their offerings of autumn fruit. But you can't drink sweat and eat scenery. We set up our scanty camp on a sandy beach and promptly ran out of ideas as to what to do next.

'Let me show you how to get clean water,' said Dave. A short distance from the water's edge, he bent down and scooped shallow depressions into the sand. After a couple of seconds, water from the river began seeping in. 'The sand acts as a natural filter and a lot of rubbish in the river will already be strained out if you dig holes like this. We'll fill up the bottles and add a purification tablet in each one. You can have a drink in about half an hour.' We followed his example and dug a line of similar holes just off the water's edge filling bottles and adding evil-smelling chlorine tablets that could make you feel as ill as any river water could.

Dave's young, tough and freckle-faced son Paulie felt free to explore. Shimmying up trees and jauntily stair-stepping over the rocky outcrop nearby, he finally came back with a large red crab claw he found. 'Here's your dinner,' he chuckled handing it over to me. I held it up and my nose and took a sniff. My stomach gave an involuntary lurch and instantly collided with my throat. The thing stank. Now my hand did also.

'Don't you want to eat it? What a little coward you are!' Paulie didn't mind. He was a natural hunter-gatherer whose skills just needed a little refining.

'If you want to eat, you'll have to catch it, kill it, dismember it and find a way of cooking it,' announced Dave with relish. Even my toes turned green and nauseous at the thought. Despite having a great love for the bush, this was when I found out how bush-oriented I really wasn't. I glanced sideways at Melan, but she was totally engrossed in what he was saying.

A motley assortment of young men went to find dry wood, grasses and things to make a fire. Dave showed us how to start a fire using the stick-rubbing-sweating-hard concentration friction method, which really only works if there is more than one person. As you rub your hands down the stick to the bottom, the next person has to start at the top to keep up the friction. We were eventually rewarded with an acrid smell and a plume of blue smoke. We started feeding it shavings, blowing gently to keep it going. Then Dave produced a smile and a box of matches.

'This was for just in case you couldn't do it. Right, gang, follow me. Time to do some exploring,' announced Dave, promptly grinding our hard-won fire out with the boot of his heel and striding off at a spanking pace and he took us on a long march-cum-run along the river's edge.

'How old do you reckon he is?' I asked Melan, puffing.

'He's quite old. Must be about 33,' she puffed back in reply. Years of exposure to the sun and smoking had not been kind to Dave's freckled face. There were loads of crinkles around his eyes and his close-cropped ginger hair seemed very thin.

Considering he was ancient *and* smoked, he could move incredibly fast and soon had a long line of youngsters strung out along the riverbank, shouting and whooping and probably sending any nearby wildlife into rapid flight. I wondered if the ones at the back really were unfit or were deliberately choosing that slow pace.

'This gives me a good idea of who is fit,' he told us as we struggled to keep up and pretending we were doing so with ease, 'and more importantly, who isn't'. He pointed out things of interest; patches of lichen, various bird species and showed us what the surrounds could teach you about the ecosystem it belonged to. It was fascinating but the only response he got was the occasional grunt. If we wanted to keep up with him, conversation was not an option.

Crocodiles make swimming in rivers dangerous, but we found a large fairly shallow pool surrounded by rocks which was safe enough for a plunge. Hot, filthy and exhausted we literally fell in and instantly revived. Bilharzia would be a problem too, but nobody really cared as long as they came out alive. Little parasites could be sorted out at random later with the use of a single dose vile-tasting tablet called Biltricide.

I climbed up a pinnacle of slippery rock and the seam on my shorts split right up to the top—beastly, disloyal things and thankfully somebody had a safety pin or I might have ended up showing a lot more than just leg for four excruciatingly embarrasing days.

Back at the campsite Dave showed us a wild fig tree full of fat green fruit which tasted horrible and a wild plum tree, covered with innocent-looking dark purple fruit guaranteed to make the mouth pucker. They were filling all the same. We shared them with spectacular fruit eating birds and an assortment of worms.

'The worms inside them had presumably only eaten fruit so they were just fruit in its protein from,' said Melan, poking around inside the fruit with a stick. I closed my eyes and just swallowed.

'There is a general rule of thumb regarding wild fruit. If it is sweet to the taste, chances are it won't do you any harm. If it's bitter, it is probably poisonous,' Dave told us. Dave knew which was which and part of the training involved teaching us. We did try a few ghastly-tasting things, but didn't swallow them, just in case.

We made a fire and sang camp songs and Dave filled us in with bush lore. Eventually the blazing African sun sank hot and liquid, below the horizon, and night fell after a very short twilight. The nightly anthem began to swell with liquid calls of various frogs, the chirruping trill of a tiny Scops owl, a fiery-necked nightjar and pearl-spotted owlet. I mention these three birds in particular because they are my favourite. Many were the nights out in the countryside where I'd listen to these hauntingly lovely sounds and been transported to a place of intensely rapturous avian heaven. All three tended to call for a short time after dusk and then again in the cool mist of predawn.

'Do you ever think of the fact that night times are a great deal noisier than day times?' asked Robert. He was a squatty little guy who flew over the rocks like a mountain goat. Things livened up a few notches when a squadron of epauletted fruit bats, with their bicycle-pump squeaks, arrived to feast off the fig tree. Dave promptly gave us a short lecture on the echo-location of bats.

From the very hot day, the night temperatures plummeted and I found sleeping outdoors extremely difficult, especially when the night is made noisy by a cacophony of snoring people and hauntingly awful sounding owls. Small wonder African people, who are more superstitious than their white counterparts, equated these owl calls with ghastly occurrences.

Several others were having the same problem and we banked up the fire, spoke quietly and listened to the cries of the deep-night owls, which I will never forget. Ever. Dave identified them all: wood owl, spotted eagle owl and giant eagle owl. Naming them naturally takes some of the mystery away and they really are magnificent birds of prey with their hot yellow eyes and unbelievably silent, gliding flight. Somewhere a hyena cackled briefly and a big cat roared. Both sounds were far enough away that they weren't a real threat. Dave had a weapon which he carried next to him all the time. My fingers itched to get hold of that gun, feel the cold wooden butt against my cheek and have a bit of target practice; I had unerring aim with a weapon even though I struggled to hold them still.

Jeremy, one outlandish character, got hold of a long, flexible stick. He rested the end in the fire until it glowed hot and red, and then gently touched the exposed flesh of some unfortunate sleeping person, who'd start wriggling and slapping at things in their sleep. Then their startled head would come up gaze bemused at the group of us still awake and Jeremy would flick the stick behind him, hiding the burning red telltale ember in the darkness behind him. There was some suspicion but no evidence. How he didn't burn anyone or set the dry brush behind him on fire, I've no idea.

The next day, earnest hunger set in. Dave headed out with a group of youngsters eager to explore, but I was assailed by indigestion. The only remedy was some bicarbonate of soda mixed with water which some thoughtful female teacher had brought along. It worked well but it took several hours for the sharp pain and off-colour feeling to subside.

'Look what we've found!' The exploration team had not come back empty-handed. In fact, they were loaded with goods, having found a poacher's camp and raided it, bringing back a cooked tortoise, wild spinach and cooked *sadza*. Tortoises are handy bush fare because they come in a ready-made cooking pot. Just dispatch them, clean them, turn them upside down and place them on the hot coals.

The best way to eat *sadza* is to squash it into little balls, dip it in relish and eat it smacking the lips to release what little flavour there is.

Being a National Parks ranger, Dave had no sympathy for these poachers, but safety was also an issue so after the meal we moved further upriver. He was the only grown man in the leadership team and the only one with a gun. The others were all female teachers from the same school as the invasion of youngsters. It was the early 1970's and also, in the back of all our minds (young and old) was the growing concern about murmurings which would eventually escalate into a full-blown civil war.

'This afternoon we can dig some holes and use this leftover *sadza* to bait traps for rats,' Dave told us. He'd had the foresight to hide some of the white stodge to prevent us eating it all. Rats and field mice could be skewered onto sticks like kebabs and roasted whole over an open fire. You could then eat them if you could stomach the stench of burning rat fur. It's a bit like burning human hair only worse.

'Who cleans up the sick afterwards?' I asked Melan.

'What sick? There won't be much in your stomach,' she replied.

Dave also taught us some basic tracking skills; something I found fascinating. Had it been possible I really think I might have made tracking my life's work. Paw prints, hoof prints and the like tell you where the game trails are as well as who has been around and where they are going. Fresh or old droppings tell you how long ago they were there. Even bent over blades of grass can tell you an animal has recently passed that way and the depth of the print can be an indicator as to the heaviness of the animal. Wind direction is also a serious consideration. You wouldn't want a carnivore to smell you before you knew it was there.

As we worked our way upstream, we had to collect frogs for the evening meal. No frog was safe. Several people hurled themselves on each one but not much is edible, only the hind legs. Melan's hat was placed on a rock and the frogs' legs spread out to dry along the brim. We bent pins into fishing hooks and used the rest of the frogs of bait them and tried our hands at fishing with some success. After a day or two of hunger, you get to the point where you are not fussy about what you will eat and that is the point Dave was hoping we would reach. I still didn't think I could eat rats, though.

After a scant lunch we headed into the water again to cool off. The laughter and splashing rapidly ceased into a stunned silence when a V-shaped wake of ripples appeared in the middle of the river heading swiftly for the bank. Amazing how such a configuration in the water can radically spoil your fun.

'Chips Out! Crocodile!' someone yelled. Everywhere, youngsters as one accord leapt out of the water and onto the safety of the rocks, aghast that we could have been sharing our pleasure time with a dangerous crocodile. All that appeared however was the head of a green, seriously ugly, prehistoric-looking but entirely harmless leguaan. Its startled head did a quick pan like a periscope, took in the rows of frightened faces and it plopped back into the green depths of the Umfuli, never to be seen again.

There was a great deal of humour especially when Robert tried to describe the size of the leguaan to Dave, but the distance between his hands kept expanding. It was obviously an expandable leguaan!

'By the way, Robert *smaaks* you,' announced the very rude Melan with relish.

'He does not, so,' I replied, suddenly feeling hot and cross. 'Besides he's a grawb,' I stalked off to find some personal space to cool down. Robert wasn't a grawb at all. In fact he was a decent, caring human being, but that he did like me was becoming painfully apparent. I was still too young to find male attention anything but embarrassing, preferring the challenges of climbing impossible-looking trees and playing with my cattie. The fact that he was decent made my observation horribly inaccurate and left me feeling guilty and ashamed.

Dave also taught us something about the stars. Using the Southern Cross as a guide and dropping a perpendicular, we could walk through the bush at night without going in circles. You have to take into account the movement of these heavenly bodies, though. It got complicated and I felt that without the actual practical side of doing the exercise I'd never really remember how to go about it.

But hunger was becoming a major issue and tempers started fraying. Having dealt with many such expeditions, Dave was expecting it and he dealt with it all by pointing out that anger and poor judgement was just as likely to cost real survivors their lives as lack of food or not knowing where they were. It was a hard lesson for us all and after that the camp seemed to fracture and people quite naturally split into groups. Melan and I, having a stronger understanding of the bush than many others, found ourselves a popular choice and the initial shyness and prejudice broke down. That was a good result, but as portrayed in books like 'Lord of the Flies' the outcome, without some control, could turn savage.

The last evening Dave dug some hidden supplies out of his Land Rover. He produced maize meal, tomatoes and onions which we cooked into a thick relish; with sweet sugar beans, tinned sausages and glass bottles of wonderful fizzy drinks so we made a veritable feast of all good things and tucked into it with great gusto made all the greater by the days of shortages.

* * *

Once the 'bush war' got underway, such jaunts naturally ended. The Army had its own Survival Camp (in places like Wafa Wafa) on the banks of Lake Kariba to the North where the soldiers training for the elitist forces went through a similar but much more harrowing experience than we did. They were allowed only two items of clothing, but were given the choice of which two (so most chose shoes and hats) in which to participate in a ten-day survival course. The instructors would not always tell the men how long they might expect to be there, thereby increasing anticipation.

There was huge emphasis on physical fitness, stamina, field craft, map reading and the ability not to panic in the face of a confrontation with the enemy when the air became hot and thick with live rounds, red and green tracer bullets, grenades, mortars and all the fire power one enemy can hurl at its rival. Sometimes unexpected tests were thrown in without warning simulating actual physical contacts. So slowly, men faced their ultimate endurance tests to the point where they became incapable of coherent thought and began acting more like automatons. It was all part of the necessary training that would make survival more likely as they would be forced to the limits of their endurance in the bush warfare with life almost completely devoid of any comfort; where cold, hunger, sudden death, mud, and war would be all they would know.

Years later (after the war ended) a Christian camp with a very similar set-up took over the old campsite. Again, the idea was a Survival Course, living only off the land, learning bush skills that would enable you to survive if nothing else was on offer. The idea was to show each participant how they would cope if life becomes stripped of all its veneer and basic necessities are all they had. People have found over time that the law is only a thin veneer that stops people from behaving badly. Out in the bush, where survival is the utmost importance and the law cannot be enforced, even the nicest people can do some really foolish things, usually out of anger or outright hostility.

When that happens, people tend to find out a great deal about themselves, what they really are made of and how much most of us actually cannot cope without life's little luxuries. When co-operation is most needed for survival it can be very difficult to show. It is then that irritations and anger can get out of hand. Everyone thinks they know best and people don't always want to work together, especially when they are with people they do not like. When someone was ill or got injured, this would increase the load on the stronger more able-bodied ones who may end up resenting this reliance.

Lawlessness and lovelessness go hand in hand. When we love others as Jesus has taught us, we will always do the right thing by them. But when lawlessness sets in, something really ugly happens to the way we treat each other. I personally hated the film 'Lord of the Flies' because this principle is demonstrated in such a savage way. Nevertheless, it contains a frightening truth about how we behave in survival situations, a truth that is not relegated to children.

Under these tough conditions, people gave their lives to Jesus because they came to the realization of just how inadequate they were under pressure. They find out in a controlled environment that lawlessness isn't necessarily something they will never fall foul of, despite what they may have previously thought. Any one of us is capable of doing great harm to others when our survival is threatened and, at any time, could fall victim to lawlessness if we do not love Jesus and do not take the time and trouble to learn how He loves others.

There are also many dangers in the bush: wild animals, hostile locals, ingesting noxious plants and illness. I remember hearing a story about one man who constantly evaded Christianity. He got dragged out of his tent one night by a lion and although he managed to escape with the help of other campers, the incident left him wounded and wary. He decided that the only way to overcome fear was to face it head on and go camping out again.

This time he got dragged out of his tent by a hyena. Unless you know Africa well, you may be tempted to think that a hyena is not as dangerous as a lion, but in fact they are. Their strong jaws are capable of breaking bones with a bite. Not only that, being scavengers, their mouths are filthy and severe infection is inevitable. It was after this second attack that the man surrendered his life to Jesus. Relatively few people ever get dragged out of their tents by wildlife but I have never heard of someone who has had to go through such an experience twice.

Finding Jesus in the land of plenty really isn't easy. When life is filled with necessities and replete with luxuries even, it is very hard for people to look into their lives and see the spiritual emptiness, the spiritual poverty they have. They are so focussed on the temporal that they cannot see the eternal. How many Christians come to a life-saving faith in Jesus out of necessity? How many times do we hear the saying, 'when He's all we have, we find out that He is all we need?' If this describes you, then why not try such a survival course? It'll change who you are and make a lot of difference to your priorities.

POTHOLES 'BELOW THE SURFACE'

THE FRAGRANCE OF BEAUTY

'Spilling a drink on a passenger is your initiation into the world of Air Hostessing,' one of the girls told me when I first started that glamorous job that was really just waitressing in the sky. Nobody actually wants to do that but holding trays of drinks amidst potential CATS (clear air turbulence) or other rough conditions that render aircraft unsteady was potential for disaster.

I only managed to do this three times, first was beer and later champagne and then cold coffee dregs. The beer and champagne victims took it all with patience and wry humour, but the coffee dregs person was very angry. Perhaps because they landed on top of his bald head and that was a sensitive spot.

Trouble with the beer was that it wasn't even the victim's drink. He looked at me with helpless appeal and said, 'Now how am I going to tell my wife I wasn't drinking?' He was, of course, making a comic reference to what he now smelled like and getting around the smell of beer is a very hard thing to do for any man whose wife might be keeping tabs on his drinking habits.

Odours or fragrances can tell a great deal about people, what they've been doing or where they have been. My work with people suffering with autism has also taught me another facet about just how crucial fragrances can be to some people. Many people with autism do not look you directly in the face. Because they cannot read facial expressions these are not nearly as significant to them as they are to people who make fuller use of their eyesight and insight into other people's characters. Wearing the same perfume and using the same shampoos is more important to people who suffer from autism because they recognise their carers by their scent as well, and so using different scent can be confusing to them, like pitching up with a different eye colour would be to someone else.

The vast majority of young men (I think it's over 60%) remember a young woman's fragrance long after they forget other things.

Fragrances can also be very evocative of past memories. Walking into a garden centre here, I was passing a stand of herbs when I smelled a pungent fragrance redolent of many happy visits to Zimbabwe's Eastern Highlands, filling me with overwhelming nostalgia. Nothing else can transport us back to other times and places as quickly as fragrances.

You can also tell a great deal about a person by the kind of atmosphere or fragrance they leave behind. Do they leave you feeling inspired? Or uplifted and filled with joy? Maybe with a new zest to go out there and conquer the day yourself! Or do they leave you feeling angry, fatigued or miserable? Or leaving you breathing a sigh of relief that they are gone?

God is the ultimate Creator and He is the only One powerful enough to create something out of nothing simply by His spoken Word, but we are all 'creators' of an atmosphere around ourselves and we tend to become known by that atmosphere. Whether you want, or even really mean to, you will leave something behind you.

The first verses we'll look at come from the Old Testament, the beautiful, poetic, and wholly romantic book, Song of Songs.

Song of Solomon 4:3
Your lips are like a strand of scarlet,
And your mouth is lovely
Your temples behind your veil
Are like pieces of pomegranate

Song of Solomon 4: 11
Your lips, O my spouse,
Drip at the honeycomb;
Honey and milk are under your tongue,

> *And the fragrance of your garments*
> *Is like the fragrance of Lebanon*

'Your lips are like a strand of scarlet' indicates sanctification through the blood of Jesus and this makes the mouth lovely! So much of our talk is not lovely and without Jesus our words are like death anyway. But a mouth sanctified by the blood of Jesus is lovely. The words of the speaker are fragrant and they are life. These verses picture the bride behind the veil and most of her beauty is hidden by that veil. The only two characteristics which penetrate the veil are her words and her fragrance.

The references to 'milk and honey' quite naturally speaks of the same words spoken of the Promised Land, a beautiful land, and both the bride and the Promised Land hold this same quality of beauty.

This is a wonderful picture of wholesome, fragrant speech, which is not optional if we are in Christ, because what comes out of our mouths reveals what is in our hearts. For James 1: 26 says, *'If anyone considers himself religious and yet does not keep a tight rein on his tongue, he deceives himself and his religion is worthless.'*

There is another amazing passage from Isaiah chapter 7 where Isaiah has had a powerful vision of the Lord, His glory filling the temple and the seraphim were worshipping Him. Isaiah's first reaction was; *'woe to me, I am a man of unclean lips and I dwell among a people of unclean lips.'* Although he was a Jew and no stranger to God, still, he became acutely aware that the words of his mouth needed cleansing. This was the first result of being in the Lord's immediate presence—the realization that what was coming out of his mouth was not holy. Our words spring (or gush or gurgle) up from our hearts, so when we are in Christ, with His righteousness as the power behind the words, we too, can achieve much with our spoken words. What an inspiration that is!

Psalm 45, which describes some of the glories of Christ and His Bride also affirm that both are made manifest with their words. Grace is poured out from the Messiah's lips, which results in the Lord blessing Him forever:—

> *'My heart is overflowing with a good theme;*
> *I recite my compositions concerning the King;*
> *My tongue is the pen of a ready writer.'*

If our hearts are also overflowing with a good theme, it will be found in our words. Our words are so important, because if we have the life of Jesus in us, we can pass it onto others with just our words! Faith comes by hearing.

2 Corinthians 2: 14-17

But thanks be to God who always gives us in Christ a part in His triumphal procession, and through us is spreading everywhere the fragrance of the knowledge of Himself. To God we are the fragrance of Christ, both among those who are being saved and among those who are on the way to destruction; for these last, the smell of death leading to death, but for the first the smell of life leading to life. Who is equal to such a task?'

(Jerusalem bible)

In Paul's day, the people were very familiar with the Roman Triumphal processions—and what an awesome display of Roman power they were! First would come the city magistrates, state officials, Roman senate and then the trumpeters. The army would follow with the generals in magnificent chariots drawn by equally magnificent horses. The ordinary soldiers would carry the spoils of victory and the banners of the vanquished enemy. Last of all would come the victims—the prisoners of war. In amongst this crowd would be musicians and priests who would carry swinging censers with incense burning in them and the entire procession would be overlaid with this powerful fragrance of burning spices. To the conquering Romans it represented the sweet, sweet smell of victory, but to the conquered it was the lingering smell of death because they would be executed before the day was over, and as a result, it probably evoked a sense of fear worse than any weapon.

As Christians, Jesus is the Head of our victory procession as we walk (or skip or run) along the Highway of Holiness behind Him. As we do, we are exuding the multifaceted fragrance of the fruit of the Spirit: love, joy, peace, patience, kindness, goodness, faithfulness, gentleness and self-control. We are His chosen warriors and we enjoy the benefits of His conquests. But do bear in mind that we manifest it first with our words.

This fragrance we exude reflects the life within us. It comes from knowing Jesus personally, living with Him a life of triumph. And very significantly, Paul says that to some people it is the sweet, vibrant fragrance of life because they are also believers and they understand and enjoy this multifaceted fragrance of the fruit of the Spirit. Whilst to others, who have rejected God it is the stench of death: signifying judgement and eternal separation from God. It may leave them feeling ashamed, guilty or even angry.

We enjoy the sweet fragrance of fellowship with other believers from our own fellowship and from other fellowships as well. One evening whilst at Nyanga, we met up with a Catholic nun who exuded such a sweet fragrance the pleasure of her presence lingered long after she had gone. She had come to Zimbabwe many years before from the U.K. to work amongst the African people. That was something worthy of respect for starters. As a white woman, far from home, on her own, working with a race and culture so different from her home country, was a very brave thing to do.

The Church had organized a piece of land, and by the sound of it, not much money. But she got together with a group of African people and they tilled the ground and planted a variety of vegetable seeds. When the vegetables were ripe, they were able to eat them and sell the overflow. With the money they earned, they purchased some chickens and began selling eggs also. The enterprise expanded to include other livestock. The money earned paid for essentials for the children. That wonderful lady left with us a fragrance we have never forgotten. We don't remember her name, exactly where her enterprise was or any specific details, except this wonderful fragrance that still brings joy at the memory of it.

Then there is the opposite effect of the fragrance, namely on those who are dying, it is the stench of death. If you want to know how open to the gospel people are, then do check their reaction to the fragrance you give off. If there are people out there who don't seem to like you, or who may be avoiding your presence, or give off some other negative 'vibe' around you, this may be the reason for it. They are reacting negatively to the life of Christ within you.

We are a sweet fragrance to God. All through the Old Testament, people made sacrifices that were a pleasing aroma to God. Today we don't need to do that anymore as Jesus has been the ultimate sacrifice, and through Him, our lives rise up to God as a pleasing aroma just because Jesus lives in us and we have faith to love and trust Him and to accept the offer He came to give.

Just as the priests of old used to burn the incense that rose up as a fragrance to the Lord, so our prayers rise to Him like incense. The Lord gathers these prayers together where He will keep them forever, for they are precious to Him. Let Jesus set your heart on fire and the fragrance of His presence will rise through your lips.

Fragrance is linked to grace. Jesus chooses clay pots to hold His lovely fragrance. We are all clay pots. What kind of clay pot were you before Jesus took you on? Were you old, young, cracked, chipped, broken, malformed, insecure, miserable, bad-tempered, lazy, anti-social, hostile, hard-working, motivated, or emotional? Or all of the above (at one time or another?), the list is endless! The point is that none of these things matter to God. He will always be willing to fill a pot no matter what its condition. This treasure, this beautiful fragrance is God's transforming grace. The pot didn't need to do anything to receive the fragrance except to be available and in need of filling. That is His free gift of grace to all of us.

We don't take this for granted. This fragrance is eternally valuable, for every drop of it came at a high cost, and that was the cross. Priceless as it is, God still wants to pour it into weak, valueless clay pots. And once the fragrance is in us, the pot becomes valuable to God. The only stipulation He has is that the pot needs to be covered with the blood of Jesus first and that comes by faith.

If you look at the Old Testament anointing oil, you will find the same thing also. It was never designed to adorn ordinary human flesh. Psalm 133 carries a picture of the anointing oil being poured on Aaron's head, onto his hair, and from there onto his beard and finally onto his clothes, without touching his flesh. This is also a picture of the fragrance in the presence of the fellowship of believers. When the fellowship of believers is united, then the anointing and fragrance will flow altogether stronger and more powerful.

However it was also associated with religious fervour. if your praise and worship are vibrant and fervent, then so will your fragrance be also. Frankincense is a resinous gum that is white and not very attractive in its natural state, but set it alight and it gives off wonderful fragrance. Burn brightly and you will smell great also and you will inspire other people to do the same.

God takes care of His people who are carrying His fragrance in the world. It is an anointing of the Holy Spirit and as such it is as rich and multi-faceted as the Holy Spirit Himself is. He is very careful with this anointing and does not waste a drop.

He also jealously guards His people who carry His treasure, because it is His anointing which makes them precious. This is also why we can say of Him: *you prepare a table for me in the presence of my foes.* It's a fragrance of victory, remember!

We are stewards of this great treasure. Notice that when our lives change because of this valuable fragrance we carry then others around us should sense the change. Hopefully once we have preached and shared the Good News, some of it will be left behind with them to carry on the work in their lives also and then God will get the glory.

This fragrance is something we cannot keep for ourselves. For fragrance, by its very nature, is something that is given off or given away. There is no way in the world you can wear a fragrance and stop others from smelling it. Like the bride in Song of Songs, two features that will always penetrate the veil are our fragrance and our words—or our fragrance in our words if you prefer.

In the book 'Dog the Bounty Hunter' Duane 'Dog' Chapman tells of a time he was imprisoned for some considerable time. He talked about the horror, hostility and hardship he encountered, and how, in the midst of all that a perfumed handkerchief made so much difference to his state of mental health. He even invited other prisoners to share that fragrance! Sometimes it is like that—in life's roughest moments just filling our lungs with wonderful fragrance can make all the difference to our wellbeing.

This exceeding greatness of God's power transcends all our weaknesses. Today I might be weak, but when I put my trust in Him, then I am strong. I might be hurting but He is my healer. Maybe I'm afraid, but He is my champion. If I am sick, then He will make me well. There may be things inside me that may cause me to be weak, but He has a remedy for them all. All I have to do is believe. And this is where there is no room for 'I am sure God will do this or that' or any ifs, buts and nevertheless type words that express unbelief. They are insulting to God who can do all things.

Further on, Paul gives us a general list of external circumstances that may threaten us as well. *'We are perplexed but not driven to despair, persecuted but not abandoned, knocked down but not destroyed.'*

This power of God that lives inside us transforms every situation, and that is what makes us more than conquerors. Without these weaknesses, Jesus' power would not be revealed. Our weaknesses and His strength work together to release magnificent, empowering grace.

Despite the chips, cracks, holes or whatever, God promises to fill our cup up until it is running over—just trust in Him to do this and that leaky old vessel will be transformed into something beautiful for God, and fill up and run over.

POTHOLES 'SHORT THOUGHTS'

FRAGRANCE AND WORDS

In the beautiful, poetic and wholly romantic Song of Songs 4: 3 we find the words:-

'Your lips are like a crimson thread and your mouth is lovely'

And a bit later on in verse 11:-

'Your lips distil nectar, my bride; honey and milk are under your tongue; the scent of your garments is like the scent of Lebanon.'

The 'strand of scarlet' indicates sanctification through the blood of Jesus, and this is what makes the mouth lovely! The bride is wearing a veil which covers her beauty and the only two aspects of that beauty penetrate the veil are her words and her fragrance. The references to 'honey and milk' are the same ones used to describe the Promised Land. Both the bride and the Promised Land have this same quality of beauty and victory.

This wonderful picture of wholesome, fragrant speech is not optional if we are in Christ because what comes out of our mouths reveals the state of our hearts. James 1: 26 says: *'If any think they are religious, and do not bridle their tongues but deceive their hearts, their religion is worthless.'* Yet how often do we speak without really thinking about it? Our words are not neutral. They either bring life or they bring death. We cannot bring life without the help of Jesus cleansing our hearts first, filling us with the pure, fresh springs of water from the washing of His word, and out of the overflow we speak words of life, healing and wholeness to others. When we are filled with the righteousness of Jesus, we cannot help but speak the words that will bring fragrance to others. There are times when we may speak these words, which may not seem significant to us, and yet they may speak powerfully into the life of another because faith has come to them by hearing.

Finally, and most important comes the promise from Revelation chapter 12 that the blood of Jesus, coupled with the word of our testimony create an irresistibly powerful spiritual weapon to overcome the enemy.

No doubt about it. Our words either bring life or they bring death. These are all good reasons to ask for deep heart fire to reach out and change the course of other people's lives! Your family and friends will thank you and the Lord, whose words are powerful enough to create a world and whose Word will stand forever, will bless you.

MEMORY VERSE:—

Revelation 12: 11
'. . . But they (the saints) conquered him (the devil) by the blood of the Lamb and by the word of their testimony, for they did not cling to life even in the face of death.'

MAY MY WORDS OF TODAY BRING LIFE
TO ANOTHER LOST OR LONELY SOUL

POTHOLES 'SHORT THOUGHTS'

THE INCY WINCY SPIDER??

The Incy Wincy Spider climbed up the water spout,
Down came the rain and washed the spider out.
Out came the sun and dried up all the rain,
And the Incy Wincy Spider climbed up the spout again.

Don't you just love the Incy Wincy Spider? Such perseverance and optimism—my guess is that the spider is the simple personification of a Christian! He was climbing up the water spout, which is what all committed Christians should do (don't tell me you've never climbed up a water spout!). It's a simple analogy about taking our life in Christ seriously.

When you do start doing that, though, that's when life's circumstances can hit you hardest and like the rain tumbling down on Incy, it can push you right back to the beginning again, testing your faith and challenging what you believe. But seasons pass, life changes and that is what we count on (see Ecclesiastes 3: 1-8). The rain stopped, as it does (even in Britain) and it's no fair contest, really. The sun has to win in due time.

Even though Incy's a small spider, he is smart enough to know when to put in his best effort—and that means waiting until all the rain has dried up—and NOT before. We ask for heavenly wisdom to shine a light on our paths and direct both our footsteps and our hearts (Psalm 119: 105). Not to be deflected from that course of action, Incy perseveres all over again with his original purpose, and that's to get back up the water spout again. Despite the setback, he returns to his purpose and goal. Setbacks should be of temporary duration only (Galatians 6: 9).

We should all be the same, really. Life has a habit of dropping awful circumstances down on top of us and pushing us down. So often we're told 'it's not what happens to you but how you deal with it that really counts' and instead of stopping at being pushed back, pray about your circumstances and wait on God for His strength and timing. Keep persevering. The top of the water spout is closer than you think, and from there, the panoramic view is earth from heaven's perspective. And it's a truly amazing sight indeed (Psalm 123: 1). By the way, Incy was also British. The weather patterns described are a give-away!

POTHOLES 'JOY BAG'

WHAT'S IN A NAME?

None of us actually like visiting the Dentist, but would you feel happier and safer in the hands of a Dentist named Dr Molar, or possibly even more appropriate, Dr Philhol?

You might find a book entitled 'Blood River' written by Tim Butcher simply must be authentic or that Lord Brain has to be the most intelligent Neurologist and Peer of the Realm that one could hope to come across. Ashley Burns is a fire fighter anyone would choose to save them from disaster and Anna Smashnova a noteworthy Israeli tennis player. Gene Shearer is an outstanding Biologist with the U.S. National Institute of Health. One thing is true of all of them—you won't forget their names in a hurry and may even be tempted to raise a laugh or two from your friends by quoting them.

The New Scientist magazine has done exactly that. Back in the 1994 after a paper on incontinence written by J. W. Splatt and D. Weedon appeared in the British Journal of Urology they popularized the idea that our names have somehow influenced key attributes of our jobs, professions or lives and they called it 'Nominative Determinism'. Naturally, the public are regularly invited to write in and share examples of Nominative Determinism that they have come across.

The sources have to be verifiable, or human beings, being what they are, may very well make up their own just for a laugh. A song entitled 'Yellow River' apparently written by I. P. Nightly or a book called 'Blob on the Wall' by Hoo Flung Dung might be amusing, but their claims to authenticity are probably spurious.

Thankfully, I wasn't a victim of Nominative Determinism as a youngster. Having the surname 'Hood' could have led me up the paths of all sorts of misdemeanours. There were times when I would give my name for something, and some wag would say; 'I asked for your *name*, not your *occupation*, dear!' or; 'And are you a hood?' and they'd peer at me as if expecting me to perform some strange antic like clean my nails with a flick knife whilst eyeing the till or be wearing a black leather jacket with a skull emblazoned across the back. My sister and I really never got that bad (honest) but our friends nevertheless produced endless nicknames relating to 'Hood' and some of them stuck.

Nowadays, though, 'hoodie' carries a much more antisocial connotation than the kind of young and silly boy-crazy goof-offs we were as teenagers. My father, christened Robin Hood by his parents whose sense of humour got the better of them, has had it even harder—although he was a pilot and never, to the best of my knowledge, robbed anyone.

The one memory which stands out was when a traffic cop in South Africa pulled us up. In those days it was not a legal requirement to wear seatbelts in a car in Zimbabwe, and all too easily we forgot that it was law in South Africa. He strolled towards the car, pad and pen in hand.

'What is your name?'

'Robin Hood,' Dad replied waiting for the ticket.

Silence. The pen remained poised a few inches in the air over the pad. The Policeman's already stern face darkened. Silent and angry, he stood there, refusing to be made a fool of but Dad and Muz sat patiently waiting, unaware that there was a problem. I had a clearer look at his face, suddenly realized why there was this awful frozen tableau and started laughing.

'You'd better not be joking,' and poor Dad very nearly got ticketed for two offences.

South African cops are not known to have a sense of humour although I am sure he went home and said to his wife; 'You'll never guess who I met today *and* he broke the law!' And of course, we all had to put up with more rounds of comments when years later, I married Jim whose father was called Tommy Tucker and he was quite little. He was shorter than me at any rate and didn't sing very often, only very loudly in Church on Sunday mornings. That's about as close to Robin Hood and Friar Tuck as one can get. Our relatives, Athol and Bobbie Field were farmers and

I grew up with Jane Hunt who became Zimbabwe's first—and probably only—female big game hunter (or is that huntress?). Leeann Rimes is a singer and Ken Bible has written some lovely hymns. Melody Green also wrote some brilliant gospel music, which was sung by her late husband, Keith Green. And who can resist applying this principle to Arsene Wenger the Manager of Arsenal Football Club?

Of course there are the examples of Nominative Determinism that are dodgy and somewhat worrying. Rod Muddle is the Head of Planning for British Airways and Frances Crook is the Director of the Howard League for Penal Reform. An article on sexual dimorphism, written by S.M. Breedlove appeared in the Journal of Neuroscience, and First Officer Coward (thankfully) brought a crippled Boeing 777 down safely preserving the lives of all on board, making him a hero.

When I initially wrote this article, it was for submission to 'Laughout' magazine, whose editor was Mr John Page. As editor of this small press magazine, he was also a victim of Nominative Determinism. I hoped he would see the funny side of it. Otherwise he might not have enjoy reading it very much. However, since 'Laughout' and its sister publications closed down that same month, the article was never published. Enjoy, and if you're a victim of Nominative Determinism, what can I say except make the most of it and enjoy reading about it even more. I did!

CHAPTER THREE

THE DAYS OF GRAIN, NEW WINE AND OIL

So came the time when the long years of war ended, the short year of Zimbabwe-Rhodesia ended and Robert Mugabe, greeted by millions of wildly applauding Africans everywhere made his famous speech of reconciliation, quoting directly from Isaiah 2: 4 the wonderful promise: 'They shall beat their swords into ploughshares and their spears into pruning hooks . . .' Many of the 300 000 (or thereabouts) white population didn't believe him, though. Who, in the history of the world, gets to change hats so radically from terrorist leader to the country's Premier (First Prime Minister then President)? Family and friends, fed up with war and its attendant horrors, the losses and the lies, the frenzied determination of this man to beat all opposition to rule this tiny, ailing and landlocked country, finally cut their losses, packed up and left for greener, more secure pastures. And in the aftershock of war, we who chose to stay behind had to deal with another grief. We had to say good-bye to many much-loved family and friends.

Humans don't have a swarming or herding instinct, but nevertheless, after the end of a war there is often a massive almost national drive towards marriage and procreation; almost as if we instinctively move to replace that which has been lost. I have read in places that many of the babies born in such circumstances are boys for the same reason.

Also, creating order out of chaos is what God Almighty did way back in the beginning, in the book of Genesis, before all this began and we all have the same characteristic in varying degrees. That's why we all enjoy doing stuff like making lists, and marking celebrations. Some of the best and happiest home-makers are the ones who enjoy restoring order to their homes after a dinner or having friends over has caused inevitable chaos. Look at the people who buy old and broken down buildings for the immense satisfaction of repairing and restoring them!

It is the same mindset that permeated the thinking of many Zimbabweans after the war. The newly-named Zimbabwe was a cesspool of exhausted, broken-down chaos. Everywhere were remnants of the war. We all shook ourselves out of shell-shocked exhaustion and began the enormous task of bringing order out of the terrible chaos. Of course, the hardest thing to restore to creativity is always the mindset of those who have been trained to fight.

When Rhodesia changed to Zimbabwe life and death remained constant companions. For whatever reason Joshua Nkomo had for leading his Zipra forces into a revolt against Robert Mugabe's Zanla forces, with their superior fighting power, it turned out to be a tragic mistake. Instead of ultimate victory, Nkomo managed to bring the whirlwind crashing down around his own head, his one-time soldiers, and of course the innocent civilians who could do nothing to protect themselves and who were once again living in terrible deprivation, as well as fear and dread of their own kind. Anyone who tried to expose these horrors became the victim of swift and savage retribution. A few years before, Ian Smith had tried to hold secret meetings with him, possibly in the hopes of these two sides joining forces against Mugabe and thereby ensuring a more balanced outcome, but of course the savagery required to shoot down innocent civilian aircraft immediately put paid to that.

These ill-advised actions resulted in the Gukurahundi massacres, also known as the Third Chimurenga where thousands of Matabeles were slain literally under the cover of darkness, and their bodies unceremoniously dumped down mineshafts in the southern region of Zimbabwe around Antelope Mine. But if the Notorious Fifth Brigade, responsible for these brutal killings, hoped that the dark and silent mineshafts could remain aloof sentinels of such a vile secret, they were wrong.

Here, in the same area where Dad and Uncle Mike had, years before, grown up free in the hot sunshine and unencumbered by any restraints of war, the word 'Gukurahundi' had once had a profound meaning, 'the winds that come before the rain and blow away the chaff' because those first rains were always a source of rejoicing. But now something terrible happened shortly after Independence. And the gold mines that had once known prosperous times and two rugged boys growing up free and unfettered in the vast expanse of land which housed them refused to hide their shameful secret. Unlike most mineshafts, which travel straight downwards, these mineshafts went straight down for only a short distance before bending at a right angle in order to follow the gold seams. When Fifth Brigade began dumping countless bodies down the gaping maws of the ancient mineshafts in order to hide the killing spree, they were unaware of the fact that those bodies would stop at that kink, clogging up the shafts quicker than they had counted on.

Nobody would wish a terrible death like that on anyone especially after the long and protracted savage war we had already fought. However, it brought the two losing sides together; the whites and the Matabeles in a now more mutual understanding of what each had been through. Although one can argue about the finer points of persecution versus betrayal, both are painfully hellacious experiences. Most Matabeles would regard these Gukurahundi massacres as betrayal by their own kind.

But for the rest of us slowly, tentatively, the lines of communication between the once-warring peoples began to open and flow. Africans began seeking higher education and better-paid jobs all of which was becoming available to them. Well-dressed African people appeared everywhere. Often, their children were dressed well enough to outstrip their white counterparts, in public at any rate. They drove smarter cars and bought houses in the lower-density (formerly white) suburbs. I'll never forget the day I apparently dialled a wrong telephone number. The voice which answered was that of a female African saying, 'Good morning.'

'Please may I speak to the Madam?' I answered in my usual stock reply presuming it was the maid who'd answered the phone. There was a short pause.

'I *am* the Madam,' came a very cold reply.

Intrepid entrepreneurs who had set up stalls on the main Harare-Kariba road became very much more inventive with their own road signs. The days of the grubby and tatty signs half heartedly advertising 'WUMS FOR SEL' disappeared. Bright white, large and clean signs advertising 'WORMS R US' or 'PUFF ADDER WORMS' or even 'WORMS LOOKING FOR A LIFT TO KARIBA' began appearing instead. Roadside stalls of bananas and oranges began appearing in and around the towns. On the long country roads other stalls with soapstone and woodcarvings became common. Many of the farms on main roads also set up roadside stalls selling fruit, vegetables and other farm produce like plants, jams, marmalades, milk and a whole variety of treats for weary travellers just longing to spend their hard-earned foreign currency.

Dad retired from flying and bought a farm near Banket, and when they set up their own roadside stall advertising 'RED WORMS OF NOTE, 100 metres' with an arrow pointing towards the stall. Some South African tourists photographed that sign which later appeared in a South African tourist magazine together with the caption: *'Are these people bragging about the size of the worms they are breeding, or what? Who on earth would buy a worm 100 metres long? What would you do with such a worm?'* to which some wag responded: *'You could always chop it into three-inch pieces and store it in bags in the deep freeze. Just don't mix it up with your spaghetti!'*

On a trip to Victoria Falls to visit a life-long friend Cathy and her husband Terry, I met Steve one night when we went to A'Zambezi River Lodge for dinner. I walked into the dining room in my new, fancy knee-length black leather boots and made a spectacular entrance by slipping and falling right on my butt. Steve, playing bass guitar in the band up at the front, quipped afterwards that I took one look at him and immediately fell for him.

Very unwisely, he asked me to marry him that night, and equally stupidly, I agreed. Steve was a committed Christian with a dynamic approach to worship and whatever else happened during the years we were married, I remember well that he was the one who finally ignited my growing faith in God, changing it from something that was simply a part of my life, to its driving force.

Steve and I became heavily involved in Church work with the Church of the Nazarene in Harare after we married in 1982, ministering to both Africans and Europeans in between working and rearing children. We, too, became torn between staying and leaving. Steve applied for a post with Air Traffic Control in South Africa but the only vacancy they were prepared to offer him was in the small mining town of Kimberley. Although we had no desire to live there, the name had huge allure and a few years later when our first baby, a gorgeous daughter was born, she was given the name Kimberley.

By its very nature, the real *agape* love of God brings out the best in people. Whatever circumstances He allows in your life, He is always looking for the best in you. If we are to be perfect reflections of His love, then this should be the underlying motive for everything we say and do to others; living and moving in such a way as to bring out the best in them also. What an awesome responsibility. It doesn't always work like that because we are confronted with quirky foibles, ill humour and we're prone to misunderstandings and even ill-timed best intentions can fall flat—and that can all happen before we even minister to another person!

Seven years and three children into marriage left Steve and I bringing out anything but the best in each other. Steve had seemingly metamorphosed into a cold and distant stranger and I was immersed in all the pressures relating to having three children under the age of four.

'I've been having an affair,' he finally admitted one night at point blank range. As I turned and fled from the room, his voice followed me, 'Do you want to know who with?' The ground suddenly titled downward and the room darkened. I clutched wildly for some support that would prevent me sliding irretrievably into that gaping, savage maw of irreversible marital damage. Of all the crass questions to ask at such a time—why on earth would I want to know the name of the co-respondent who was destroying my marriage?

The eternal triangle is a common enough relationship-killer and it gets plenty of publicity, but personally I will never figure out why a troubled spouse might think that the introduction of a third person into the mix might somehow provide a suitable answer for all parties concerned. So I learned that grieving cycles can be triggered off by circumstances other than death. And yet looking back in the days that followed, I could see how the Lord had prepared me for what was coming and I was able to forgive Steve as an act of my will in the power of the Holy Spirit despite the maelstrom of emotions raging within. No, it wasn't a once-off forgiveness and then I sailed off into the sunset complete with sundowner and braai'd spare ribs. Some days the hostility and anger kept seeping in and I had to keep forgiving him.

So we ride that wave of grief and optimistically look forward to the day when life returns to normal so that we can get on with the business of living. But it is never the same again. We are never the same again. Although we both tried to heal the breach, it never really worked. The very nature of betrayal makes restitution almost impossible and we parted company two years later.

During this time I encountered a precious supernatural miracle from the Lord. Divorce is frowned upon by the Church, and in one sense, understandably so. Marriage and the family is God's original idea, implemented in the beautiful garden planted by His own hand and all before the Fall of the human race. It was meant to be a perfect reflection of the constant exchange of love that occurs between the three members of the triune Godhead. When it works well, it is a reflection of heaven on earth. When it falls apart, it is a tragedy whose ripple effects may well affect future generations. We aren't meant to get divorced, that's true. But sometimes we take God's word much further than He ever intended it to go and we make divorce the second most unforgiveable sin. Divorcees, like everyone else, are under the good rain of God's grace, and nothing we do can change that.

So one night when I was praying alone I said to the Lord, 'Lord, I know that You still love me, but right now You feel so far away.' I felt dreadful, like I'd just slain an injured animal that could have been saved.

The next day as I was dropping Kimberley and Robin, my middle son, off at Alpha-Omega school, a young teenaged girl approached me. I knew her name was Tara Pierson and that she was the daughter of the school Principal. 'As I was praying last night, the Lord gave me a message to give to you. He told me to tell you that He is very close to you,' she said to me. And she gave me some scripture verses to verify this word of knowledge.

One of them was Psalm 34: 18; *'The Lord is near to those who have a broken heart, and saves such as have a contrite spirit.'* Another was the dramatic scene from Acts chapter seven where Stephen said, *'Look! I see the heavens opened and the Son of Man standing at the right hand of God!'* When Jesus entered heaven, He *sat down* at the right hand of God the Father. When Stephen stood up for Him, He also stood up for Stephen. Amazing God, amazing grace that He in turn would stand up for those who would honour Him. For me it was a turning point. And so, through the faithfulness of someone who barely knew me, the Lord spoke the words of healing that began the rebuilding of my life.

Since then I have suffered two other serious betrayals; both of have resulted in severe loss which has necessitated the rebuilding of my life. As write this, I am not sure that there are any lessons about betrayal that I have not already learned. But if you want to be in any kind of Church leadership, you will find that persecution and betrayal are practically prerequisites to such a position. They are almost bound to happen.

People who love us also have a great deal of knowledge about us. Should they choose to betray us, then that knowledge could be used to damage our credibility. In some circumstances it can even be dangerous—which is why desertion from the army is always treated as a very serious offence. Desertion, denial and betrayal are all loops in the same downward spiral, varying only in intensity but not in kind.

Yet at the same time, I'm sure that there are many, many things that Almighty God still has to teach me in all life's experiences—recalcitrant pupil that I am! One of them is the incredible joy He gives us in the face of disaster. Nehemiah once wrote: *'The joy of the Lord is my strength'* and if that is where strength is derived from then that's the greatest way to get strong—especially in the face of life's major disasters. He has also taught me that order out of chaos can apply to a severely damaged relationship, and that if and when reconciliation occurs, He can restore a relationship to something infinitely better, more solid than it ever had been before.

After the heartbreak, years of change and growth came. Life as a divorcee began with a few months of recovery time on the parents' farm and then that rainy December 1991, I was able to move into Gran's house in Miller Road, Borrowdale, a classy suburb on the northern side of Harare. The rains had come early and everything smelled great. There's no smell on earth which brings relief quite like that of refreshing rain, bringing burgeoning new life, emerald green bushveld and lawns and sends everything into a growing frenzy. Gran herself relocated to a Retirement Village in the farming district of Bindura.

The folks found a maid called Dorcas, a sweet natured young Christian woman with two small children. Muz told me afterwards we were like two ragamuffins, two women both with children to look after and no one to help and little experience to help us with the challenges that lay ahead.

We moved all our stuff, with the help of Dorcas and Patrick, the gardener who'd worked for many years for my Grandmother. The children sorted out their rooms; Kimberley's was all pink and green mix-and-match and the boys' had blue and gold Asterix curtains. And after the heavy work was over, I loaded a tray with tea, cool drink and cakes and took it out into the garden.

The house, designed in an L shape basked in the golden glow of the late afternoon sunshine, and inside the L was a lovely sun catcher patch of emerald green lawn. Watching the children running around and exploring their new environment with delight sent fresh pangs through me, and it was as if the next twenty years opened up before me, all years where I may well be looking after them on my own. What had I done? What had I let myself in for? How on earth was I going to cope? I didn't have that level of capability. Lord, what, oh what, am I going to do. I burst into tears.

Read Psalm 118: 5 was the thought that came into my head, and as my bible was inside the house, I rose to get it. The words quickened to my soul:—

'I called on the Lord in distress;
The Lord answered and set me in a broad place'

It was a moment outside of time, as I felt the layers of pain, anger, guilt, shame and grief unzip and slide away from me like a garment. I had cried out to the Lord, and He had indeed answered—by setting me free. I still didn't know how I was going to manage, but I was no longer afraid because I wasn't alone. The Lord was not going to hold a failed marriage against me. Little did I realize then just how magnificently the road would rise up to meet me in the days ahead.

The second miracle occurred shortly afterwards when I started looking for a job. Trying to juggle financial figures was difficult, and the realization that working full time was not a viable option because I would have to pay some crèche to look after the children in the afternoons, I began to look for that rarity called a 'morning's only' job. A friend, Richard Tasker, who was working for an employment agency, found me one with The Discount Company of Zimbabwe.

'You're in luck,' he told me happily over the phone. 'They had already employed someone else in the job, but shortly after she started a close relative of hers who lived overseas became seriously ill and she had to fly over. She told them not to keep the job open for her. I'm going to send only you for an interview and I'm hoping they'll just give you the job.'

As I got ready for the interview, tears kept trickling down my cheeks. Starting out a new life on my own just felt so awkward and so uncomfortable. I had spent five years at home with the children and all my office skills desperately needed brushing up. Would they have me?

'Do you know anything about the money market?' Mr Helby asked me during the interview.

'No, I'm afraid not. I'm also newly divorced so I might be a little emotional from time to time, but I have people skills and I can type. I'm also very willing to learn.' I was honest with him, in the hopes that if I honoured God, then He would also honour me and I returned home to await the phone call to tell me I had the job. There I was to meet and work closely with Deidre Bawden, a lovely blonde lady, all soft cotton and rich velvet, who spoke Shona like a local and who became a great friend. Rita Wilson, who was leaving and whose position I filled, popped in from time to time, a surprising lady whose external austerity hid the most surprisingly wicked sense of humour I have ever come across.

We had not been in our new house long when I decided to try Highlands Presby Church. On the Sunday morning we dressed in our best and went to the first service, only to find the service was more 'business' than ministering to the congregation. Evidently, the senior Minister had done something which required disciplining and would be leaving the Church with immediate effect, leaving the lay workers to run the Church until a replacement was found. I slid a little further down into the seat and blew out a sigh, not sure if this was really the place for someone whose own life needed rebuilding in the warm, safe environs of a strong Church. But who am I to question what I thought Almighty God might have in mind?

I decided to cast a fleece before Him, and filling in a Visitor's Questionnaire form, I placed it in the collection plate with the prayer, *If they visit me before Friday, then I will know this is the Church You want me to be in.* And I left it like that.

The following evening, someone telephoned from the Church to ask if they could pay a visit that Thursday evening. The fleece was answered. I couldn't change my mind and go somewhere else. And so began what I call the Days of Grain, New Wine and Oil; days when the Lord blessed us in many ways. From a distance of many years now, I look back upon them as the happiest days of my life.

When the team came on Thursday evening, it was actually part of their evangelical outreach, and when they found out that I was already a Christian, they asked if they could just practice on me. So I met Kurt, Alaine and Val.

'Before we go any further though, I want you to know that I am divorced. If this is a problem for your Church, then please tell me now. I don't want to start going to your Church and then find that this is a problem.' Cheeky and forthright, but I needed to know.

'There are seven divorcees in the housegroup I attend,' Alaine replied. That settled it. I'd meet them all in due course and we would together explore the difficulties and challenges that lay within being both single and parents—not quite fitting into the singles group because we had children and not quite fitting into the married couples with children group because we were single.

A few weeks into my new life, one particular night stands out in my memory. I had switched out all the lights, and then stood by the bedroom window in the dark. I drew the curtains back and looked outside into the night sky with its bright stars. Africans were walking along the road talking quietly. The squeaking trill of crickets came from the newly-mown grass, the scent of which wafted up to me alone there in the dark. The days were full and satisfying and yet there was still sharp emotional pain deep inside. *The joy of the Lord is your strength*, the thought floated gently into my conscious mind. *Jump on your sorrow with both feet. Jump on it; press it down hard until it is out of sight.* It seemed a hard call, but then again, when it's a question of faith, the waters don't part until our feet get wet. I trusted God the Holy Spirit that night and sure enough, the pain began to ease.

Divorcees are sometimes referred to as 'the thirty-something-year-old-teenagers'. In those first few months I understood why this was so. Firstly, God had graciously led us to a new home, a new job, a new church and so He began replacing that which was lost. Then one night my long-time friend Lynne Ellis phoned me.

'I've left Rob,' she said. 'I need a place to stay.'

'Come and stay with me until you find your feet again,' I suggested and I rearranged our new home to accommodate herself and her young son, Scott. Like Timothy, Scott had a tendency to get into mischief. Kimberley moved into my room and the boys moved into Kimberley's room, leaving theirs free for Lynne and Scott. Scott and Timothy were born within a few months of each other; both had blue eyes and lots of woolly blonde curls (well until they got hold of a pair of scissors one night and cut each other's hair leaving a trail of golden curls on my scarlet carpet).

Lynne arrived in her little grey Renault, and for some inexplicable reason, the back seat was loaded to the gunnels with toilet rolls.

'Cool! But what are we going to do with all those loo rolls?' I asked.

'Don't make me tell you what toilet paper is for!' Lynne giggled.

Gale-force laughter bellowed out almost immediately, and so began a few months of irrepressible, mischievous thirty-something-year-old teenagers, complete with air guitars and raucous singing. Laughter rang out again and again over those months, and how healing it was, too! Lynne, with her mass of cloudy dark hair and infectious laughter, livened up the evenings and weekends considerably.

In the meantime, we began attending Highlands Presby church and it didn't take us long to realize that most of the young people attended the evening services, complete with Praise and Worship band, lots of music, the Word and regular miracles and Holy Spirit ministrations in the services. Praise and Worship, with great choruses, usually last around half an hour and was usually followed by a time of open prayer. Then the Youth Leader gave the word. At the time, the Youth Leader was Andy Shaw and he remembered me from a few years back when his sister Alison Desmond had introduced us. Andy's messages were dynamic. In the evening the Church was so full that late-comers sat on the stairs, and in the choir stall. They stood in the entrance way and sometimes outside on a hot summer night. The place was crowded the music reverberated to the heavens, quite literally. I am still sure I heard angels singing along with us, notes impossibly pure and high for humans. I am also convinced that these angels could sing in chords, whereas we humans can only produce a single-note sound. Afterwards, we either stayed in the sanctuary and prayed alone or with others or had tea and cakes and socialized a lot.

One of the things I started doing was joining the Evangelical outreach programme as a praying partner for Kurt. One evening we gathered at the Church for prayer as the teams went out. Whilst we were praying, I felt a dreadful heaviness descend on me, cloying and disgusting. I almost gagged.

When the teams returned and gave their reports, Kurt drew me aside. 'Did anything happen whilst you were praying?' he asked. The question might have seemed strange, but he was obviously aware that all was not well.

'Actually it did. I felt this awful sense of heaviness come over me.'

'We saw it.'

'Saw what?'

'Saw the demon. When we approached one house to go in, we saw this incredibly bright, beautiful being materialize out of nowhere. At first we thought it was an angel, but then it turned around and it had the most hideously ugly face I've ever seen. We got a horrible fright.' Satan and his cohorts were once angels of light, and they could still appear as such.

Kurt still looked a bit shaken. I thought that was the end of it, but I was wrong.

The period of mischief and fun with Lynne didn't last all that long, perhaps three months at the most. It came to a natural close when Charlie Canning and his wife Lynne who belonged to Northside Community church and also ran a Christian band called 'Yadah' called.

'We've been going around schools giving concerts and we're looking for someone to start a counselling/encouragement type team to handle the altar calls when the music's finished. Andy Vaughan recommends you wholeheartedly. Are you up for the job?' he asked me. Was I up for the job? Absolutely! Already visions came crowding into my head, ideas jostled for space in my mind which was already racing ahead and conquering the world. What an invitation! To be able to do something like that for God, to be able to give something back into the community and to Him for all that I had been through was a tremendous gift.

The first school holidays in April rolled around and it was decided that the children would spend some time with their father and his new wife, plus some time on Tumbleweed Estates with my parents. As much as I wanted them with me, they had other people to visit, other interests to cultivate and other things to do. The rain tailed off and the hot sunshine grew cooler. April was always my favourite time of the year, not only because of my birthday, but because of the weather—endless days of warm, dry sunshine, ripening crops and a sense of the fullness of summer replete.

But this time, for the first time in my entire life, I was alone in the house. I gave Dorcas and Patrick extra time off to relax and do their own thing and I struggled, as every divorcee must do, to make the transition from loneliness to aloneness. There is a wealth of difference in the two definitions behind the words. Loneliness is like the scourge of humankind, designed and created for fellowship as we were. Aloneness, on the other hand, can be a rich experience where we can spend time on our own assimilating our lives, doing the things we really just enjoy doing, catching up with God and with ourselves. Although I have always been something of a loner, those first few weeks were very hard indeed.

Each evening, when I closed up the house and locked the doors, I was alone—all by myself—until Dorcas, smiling and cheerful, came in the following morning. If it was a weekend or time off for her then she was not there as she usually visited her home in Banket.

Then during the night something scary and horrible began happening. I was woken up regularly by some strange demonic entity. I could feel its presence pestering me and mocking me for the loneliness. I could feel it poking and prodding me as though trying to find a point of entry. Although I was not afraid, it became a serious irritant. I didn't need any reminders that I was alone, and I certainly didn't need any demons around in my new life.

I rebuked it, and it disappeared. But each time, it would return and always when I was alone. Why was that? I mused. I thought we could cast these things out and they went away. But not this one, and although I sensed that it was not a demon of any great power or strength, I couldn't seem to get rid of it. Frustration increased until I found out about Yvonne Gentleman.

'You need to visit Yvonne Gentleman,' Margie told me. 'She really does have a number of supernatural gifts in the Holy Spirit including the ability to cast out demons.' I knew Yvonne from way back—she had been a great friend of my Gran's.

I'll never forget that first visit. The elderly, gentle-natured lady who sat opposite me had the most piercing, pale, light-blue eyes I had ever seen and they pierced my being right down into the depths of my soul and nothing was safe. She would know everything; including the things I didn't tell her. I was desperate to hide from that gaze; it was not comfortable.

'I think there may be a curse somewhere along the line that we need to break,' she said at length, when I finished telling her about this demonic entity. 'It sounds like a semi-physical demonic manifestation. Has anyone in your family been involved in the occult? Ever been to a fortune-teller? Are there any Christ dishonouring things in your home?' She asked a series of questions designed to give her the information she needed—somewhere along the line there was an opening to the demonic realm. We needed to pray and ask the Lord to close it.

Apart from a ridiculous visit to a fortune-teller many years ago, I couldn't think of anything specific; there weren't any major skeletons in the family closets although like most families, we did have our secrets. Then I remembered the incident at the Church, the spirit of heaviness and the spiritual hornets' nest we had apparently disrupted and so I told her about it.

'Let's pray,' said Yvonne. She was the kind of Spirit-filled woman who did not need to ask too many questions of the person who came for help. Anything she needed to know, she relied totally on God to supply that information. There were times when she came up with something I desperately needed but had not told her about. Yvonne prayed in English and in tongues. She slashed the air above my head and finally ended on a note of delight.

'I've just had a vision of your guardian angel chasing the demon. Great sight, as always! Now, there are two more things. The demon will try and make a come-back. These things don't give up easily if they can possibly help it. Next time, you take authority over it and cast it out and it won't be a problem anymore. The second thing is after the divorce you need to go home and pray over your children and ask the Lord to break the soul ties. Sins of one generation tend to get handed down to the next, so they need to be broken. Legally, if you are all Christians, then in Christ all curses are already broken but sometimes, such as in a case like this, it is better to pray specifically and ask the Lord to break those ties.'

I thanked her and walked out. I was going to be interested in how this would pan out, having never deliberately taken authority in the name of Jesus into the spiritual realm. But I was ready for a fight.

It happened a few days later when I was driving home from housegroup at Honeydew Farm and Mike and Sandy's lovely home. Driving through the darkness, punctuated at regular intervals by gleaming orange street lights, I could feel something cold and slimy slide down around my throat from the rear of the car and begin trying to choke me.

'"*Behold I dwell under the shelter of the Most High God,*"' I spoke the words out loud, quoting Psalm 91 from memory. The effect was instantaneous, as quickly as one would withdraw one's hand from a hot stove. The pesky thing had been given a good slap and it never returned.

When the children returned, I took the first opportunity to put Yvonne's instructions into actions. It was early one Saturday morning. The early sun, still weak and watery, seeped in the lounge windows, bringing out the rich tones of the same luxurious Axminster carpet I had once laid down on as a child. It was still in good condition, except for a couple of ugly gashes some 'Bright Light' had inadvertently made with his FN years before. I sat down with the children and explained what I was about to do. Because there were three of them, I had Timothy in my lap, Robin on my left and Kimberley on my right. I placed each hand across two shoulders and prayed, 'Lord, in Your name, I pray for these soul ties to be broken.' Again, the effect was immediate and physical as all three children simultaneously jerked under my hands. I was so startled that I stopped praying and opened my eyes and stared, amazed.

Setting up an encouragement/counselling team for 'Yadah' was full of challenges and became one of life's richest, most uplifting experiences. As I write this, I found a notation in one of Kimberley's old diaries that read: 'Mom was expecting ten people for house group and only six turned up. She wasn't very happy'. I look back on that and smile. That was only the beginning and it moved on upwards from there. 'Yadah' band members attended Northside Community Church and the support team came from Highlands Presby. There was a couple from Church of the Nazarene, so it also became something of an inter-church outreach.

The young singles group at Highlands Presby was large for Harare—somewhere in the region of 500. We all streamed in on a Sunday evening, filling the pews, choir stalls, the three long staircases leading down to the front until there was standing room at the back only. It was from here that I found a large number of youngsters on fire for God and keen on joining the group. Eventually we began sitting together in the pews and I met and became friends with a lot of singles who all became special to me.

As the Monday evening group grew to around 20 at its best, so the format for the evening began to change as people started arriving at about 5.30 pm for tea and a chat—it was always best to get the chatting out of the way first. Serious bible study and talks on counselling and encouraging others followed, after which we all had dinner together. After dinner, those who wanted to leave were free to do so, but many stayed on for prayer. These sessions were often blessed with the Lord's immediate presence and would often carry on until late. The children sometimes joined us for the early part of the evening and Dorcas always made an excellent meal. Despite her lack of experience, she was a naturally gifted cook.

Peter Lorimer, tall, dark-blond and somewhat enigmatic, could play the guitar and he led us in praise and worship. The singing was a delight to my soul, making me feel cleansed and refreshed and ready for more service.

Well do I remember that first 'Yadah' concert we attended, and how I loved their music—songs that would bring a lump to my throat no matter how many times I heard them. Resplendent in our scarlet tee shirts, we'd sit at the back waiting until after the music ended and the altar call was given.

Several youngsters made their way to the front and sat down to wait. I approached one young African girl and sitting next to her, I asked, 'You've come up to the front for help. Is there anything I can help you with?'

She looked at me with those sad brown eyes and replied simple and straightforward with, 'My brother has a demon.' Whoa! I'd been thinking in my mind: 'teenagers equates to problems with parents, peers, alcohol, drugs, sex, identity or self esteem.' I didn't have much to prepare me for this one, except that which I'd undergone in the School of Hard Learning.

'Umm, hasn't he got any simpler problems? Is everything alright at home? What about his relationship with your parents?'

'Yes, everything else is okay.'

'Are you sure?'

She was sure. I had some scanty knowledge of deliverance and demonology from my own experience and I looked up some scriptures and we prayed together.

'Can I have your name and address?' I asked her. I needed to look up some things and write to her. After she had given them to me, I looked around for other members of my team who were free and we all prayed for her.

Deliverance and demonology was something I was going to learn in the hard school of experience—and not because I had any great desire to be there, either.

One particularly frightening experience occurred up at Nyanga during a family weekend. Nyanga was in the beautiful Eastern Highlands of Zimbabwe, a place of crisp, cool air overlaying pine and wattle forests, clear cold streams filled with trout from the Hatcheries. There we took long rambling walks collecting dried pine cones for the fire. The mountain range is steep and much of it wooded with trees not indigenous to the area. The highest peak, Mount Nyangani wasn't difficult to climb. The first stage was very steep, but for the rest it was a long, gentle slope to the summit. However, you had to stay on the path demarcated by white cairns. The mountain was shrouded in mystery as much as in mist and some strange disappearances have occurred on its heights—tragic disappearances that have yet to be explained or brought to a logical conclusion.

Udu Dam, not far from its base housed one of a number of National Parks cottage sites. All the National Parks sites were built around such dams: Mare, Rhodes and Udu. Dad, Mom, and Kimberley were sharing a cottage and Robin, Timothy and I were sharing another one along with Melan, Carly and Tammy. Robin (then aged ten) was sleeping on a spare bed in the lounge and during the night he came through to me.

'Mom, I've had a bad nightmare, please can I sleep with you?' I moved over so he could get in, but it was strange. Robin had never once been bothered enough by nightmares to disturb me. After a while he fell asleep, but I did not. The bed, being National Parks issue, was far too narrow for two, so once he was asleep; I slipped out and moved to his bed in the lounge. I hadn't been asleep long, when I found myself startled out of sleep and suddenly absolutely petrified for I was not alone in that room. I found myself head-to-head with the most vicious demon I had come across in my limited experience. The impression wasn't so much of overwhelming evil, although that was present. It was the sense of terrible hatred bent on destruction that emanated from that being, and once again found myself in the clinches of a demon trying to throttle the life-force out of me.

Suddenly petrified and in fear of my life, all I could think to do was cry out, 'Jesus, HELP!' No bible verses sprang to mind, just a simple agonized plea. The room flooded with blinding light for an instant and then there was a sense of complete peace. The fear had gone instantly along with the protagonist who had inspired it. I didn't bother to turn on a light although the night was pitch dark, sensing that the battle was over and the victory complete. Turning on a light might have broken that calm, peaceful sensation as it would have suggested a lack of faith.

I found that although the biblical directives for dealing with these despicable entities is always the best role model for us to follow, nevertheless God is the author of creativity and you can use other spiritual weapons just as effectively. After one particular deliverance I sang a few lines from one of Carman's songs:—

'I love Jesus yes I do,
I love Jesus,
How about you?'

Whatever the demon was, it scarpered; praise and worship of God is complete anathema to such a being. But in all these occasions, it became very clear that when Ephesians talks about the hierarchical structure within the demonic realm, it is very real. Some demons were more of an irritation and didn't appear to have any real power whereas others had power and they were dangerous, vicious and totally bent on destroying whatever they could in our lives. It pays to always remember that they are already *defeated* powers because that is what Jesus accomplished on the cross, even if they don't want to behave that way.

After a few months, Lynne and Scott found their own place and moved out. For a time, we were on our own and then Geraldene Prescott moved in—my house was simply an in-between-moving-home-and-finding-my-own-place for her. Here she had a taste of recalcitrant children and loud music very early in the morning. She tells me that she still remembers all the words to Petra's *'Unseen Power'* album and some of David Meece's amazing music, too. Bryan Adam's 'Everything I do' had topped the charts and we sang it regularly and often, two single women casting careful eyes around for just one God-given Knight. Geraldene was a totally domesticated and a talented lady in many respects, also had an amazing voice. I always thought that the man who would eventually marry her would want for nothing in his home.

Over time some of the older members; Chris Parry, Chris Saint and Lawrence Trim all became leaders one way or another. Today, memories of their wisdom, their life's experiences and their humour are still amongst my most cherished.

Yvonne Gentleman spent a couple of Monday nights leading and teaching our group. What nights those were!

'I've made the verses from Isaiah chapter 61 my life's work,' she told us. We read it together:—

'The Spirit of the Lord is upon Me,
Because the Lord has anointed Me

To preach good tidings to the poor;
He has sent Me to heal the broken-hearted,
To proclaim liberty to the captives,
And the opening of the prison to those who are bound;
To proclaim the acceptable year of the Lord,
And the day of the vengeance of our God;
To comfort all who mourn in Zion,
To give them beauty for ashes,
The oil of joy for mourning,
The garment of praise for the spirit of heaviness;
That they may be called trees of righteousness,
The planting of the Lord,
That He may be glorified.'

It took me a long time to appreciate how the power-filled anointing of the Holy Spirit is for ministering to others. We are channels of that particular blessing—it was never meant to be kept but shared. As far as I may be able to tell what could possibly be on the mind of Almighty God, I am convinced He blessed our counselling group with these magnificent power-gifts because we were seeking to minister to others, to build them up and give them a chance at something better, new life in Christ.

We saw legs grow out that evening, my own included. How strange to be thirty plus years old and not notice that one leg was slightly longer than the other! But it was, and Yvonne, kneeling down in front of me, took my feet in her hands and prayed whilst one lengthened. It took away back pain for many years—and what a blessing that was!

Jo Ades turned to Yvonne and said to her, 'You have had a pain in your foot for a long time.'

'Yes I have,' replied Yvonne, and as Jo prayed for her, the pain was healed and to the best of my knowledge, never returned.

The children used to come to concerts whenever they could, Robin with a natural ear for music and an excellent sense of rhythm, became very interested in drumming. They'd stand at the back, play and sing and became known as 'Mini Yadah' much to the enjoyment of the real 'Yadah' up onstage who could watch these youngsters mirroring their actions.

POTHOLES 'BELOW THE SURFACE'

REST IN INHERITANCE

Throughout the last fifteen or so years of studying grace, I have found that there are a number of different ways of expressing the same thought, as long as all are rooted and grounded in the Person of Jesus Christ:—

- The Law and grace were both foreshadowed by the two trees in the Garden of Eden: the Tree of the Knowledge of Good and Evil from which the Law finally came and the Tree of Life which is prefigures Jesus Christ and finds its fulfillment in the book of Revelation.
- The bible also talks about 'rest in inheritance' which parallels salvation with rest.
- The book of Hebrews contrasts 'the shadow' with 'the substance'—'the shadow' being the Old covenant based on the Law which was given to the Levites through the priesthood of Aaron and grace being 'the substance' foreshadowed by the mysterious Old Testament character, Melchizedek. The order of priesthood which would come through Jesus Christ and the line of Judah is the same as Melchizedek and not Aaron.
- There are references in the New Testament to being 'in Christ' or the 'fullness of Christ.'
- All of which basically have the same meaning: grace.
- GRACE is often referred to as 'God's Riches AT Christ's Expense'

- GRACE is also often referred to as 'GRACE is God At Work'

In Genesis, the first thing Adam and Eve noticed when they sinned was that they were naked—and they became ashamed of it. Although the reference is to physical nakedness, I think the essence of that shame was much deeper. It referred to a spiritual nakedness as well.

That's why the covering of fig leaves would never, ever suffice. It was the work of their own hands, a covering that will always be inadequate, and it only took care of their immediate physical needs. Spiritually, they were still naked, vulnerable to one another and open to further satanic attack, human relationships were fractured and people felt the first negative emotion: fear.

God in His infinite wisdom and mercy took the life of a blameless animal and covered them with skins. Sin took life and life had to be taken to cover that sin, but only in the work of the Creator's hands was sufficient to cover all their nakedness, physical as well as spiritual.

Have you ever noticed how much more vulnerable you feel when talking about matters of the spirit? That's because we humans are spiritual beings, and whether we believe in God or not, does not alter the fact that it is in spiritual matters that we are the most vulnerable.

When we strive to cover this nakedness with our own good deeds, it won't work. It will never work. *'All your righteousness is like filthy rags,'* Isaiah tells us. This kind of clothing is insufficient and pointless in the presence of a holy God.

I also think that this is why people may have a tendency to feel insecure about their beliefs, to the point where they become extremists and, like Cain, some of them will resort to murder. It's a large part of the reason why false religions will always have a tendency to produce murderers whilst the one true religion will produce martyrs.

When we come to this realization, and we come to God for salvation, the blood of Jesus covers us with forgiveness, the water of the Word washes us and the garment of salvation covers us. This means that whenever God the Father looks upon us, He sees the blood of His precious Son Jesus and that's what makes us acceptable to Him.

This is the garment that allows us to come into His presence, acceptable in His sight. The first garment we are given is the garment of salvation and it is an undergarment.

With salvation comes rest. God worked for six days and then entered into His rest. When we become Christians we enter into God's rest first. I think you will find that if you look up in your Concordance all the words for 'rest', 'salvation' and 'inheritance' that they are often intertwined and interlinked. God's rest is His salvation and His salvation is rest and that is part of the wonderful inheritance He has given us.

But salvation is only an undergarment. From there, it gets even better! There are other God-given garments that we need to wear in order to ensure that we are strong enough to walk in the world, and stand before the enemy. Pointless relying on our own strength when we can have such amazing strength in Jesus!

Isaiah chapters 61 and 62 are very interesting. *'Put on the garment of praise for the spirit of heaviness.'* I am sure that the vast majority of human beings suffer from depression from time to time, and even as Christians we can still be affected by depression, especially in trying times when things go wrong, great losses are suffered or when life takes a downturn.

Depression can sometimes be a physiological reaction to suffering. The 'feel good' hormones released in our brains—the serotonin and dopamine levels can drop causing a feeling of depression.

It has been pointed out to me that a 'spirit of heaviness' can also be satanically inspired attack. And the scriptures give us a remedy. *'Put on the garment of praise for the spirit of heaviness.'* No devil is going to hang around a person praising God—that just makes a horrible atmosphere for them.

On several occasions when we have been privileged enough to deliver someone from a demonic presence, we have always advised them afterwards to create and keep around them an atmosphere of praise and worship, play hymns and praise music because evil spiritual forces will not want to hang around that kind of atmosphere.

In the passage from Isaiah, we also hear about the *'robe of righteousness.'* Once we are seated, the next step is learning to walk like a Christian in the world. For this we have been given a *'robe of righteousness'* to cover the garment of salvation.

Salvation and righteousness act as light for the rest of the world. People who are not saved are walking in spiritual darkness, and simply by the presence of a Christian in their lives, they are being exposed to God's light. Let us pray that they are attracted to that light.

Christmas has become extremely commercialized, and one of things that we are robbed of in this day and age of breakneck pace is rest. If you look at first world countries today, many shops are open 7 days a week. Many of the bigger stores are open 24 hours a day. It never fails to amaze me in England that no matter how small or obscure the road you are on, there are always others on that same road, especially when you are on the wrong road, and you want to make a u-turn around somewhere—there's always someone behind you blocking the exit.

The one characteristic above all others that sets Jews apart from all other nations is their Sabbath rest. I know that the Mosaic Law was only given to Jews and it was given for a limited time period only—until Jesus ushered in the new covenant of grace. And yet, if you examine the entire Law and not just the Ten Commandments, its underpinning principles are ones that make for a healthy, balanced lifestyle, and regular periods of rest were a part of that lifestyle.

Years ago, we were privileged to have a Jewish friend, Lawrence Trim, who invited us to their Friday night 'Shabbat' or Sabbath meal. The children were also invited because Shabbat is a family meal. And we thoroughly enjoyed those evenings, aside from the wonderful food. They are 'love feasts' where families are together and the conversation must always be edifying to God.

If you are ever in Jerusalem on a Friday evening, you will hear the Sabbath horn sounding at sundown, and noisy, busy things like construction sites and public transport close down for the Sabbath and a blanket of silence and peace falls over the city. I doubt if any other city in the world enjoys this cessation of noise on a Friday evening! The Jews take their rest seriously and everything slows down to a blended wholeness of peace. They have worked tirelessly during the day to prepare for the Shabbat, especially the women who are wives and mothers. They have to make sure everything is ready before that horn sounds, and then comes the most important evening of the week, when they always serve the best meal. Even the poorest of Jewish families will do their best to serve a good meal for Shabbat.

The children dress up in their best clothes and spend the evening with their parents. In the synagogues on a Sunday, the women may be segregated, but on a Friday evening, they are queens of their own home.

People of the world cannot know true rest, because true rest belongs to God. They will always be vulnerable to 'peace—not as the world give' otherwise known as RESTLESSNESS. Youngsters, especially as they get older dress up to go out and spend Friday nights with their friends. Parents catch up on work, watch TV or go out themselves. Many families live on fast food, because that's the only food that fits in with their fast-paced lifestyle.

Then Ephesians chapter 6 details another, totally different set of garments—the armour of God that allows us to stand before the enemy. Each piece of that armour is detailed and has a purpose. I won't go into detail here, but I do know people who daily pray over each item of that armour and they are ready to face anything the day might throw at them. Whether we like it or not, we have a very real enemy, the devil, and he will do anything to stop us from believing, receiving and living in God's grace, in the power and person of Jesus Christ because then he will be afraid of us. When we are living in the power of the risen Christ, we are living in the power that defeated him long ago, before the foundation of the world the sacrifice was made that would ultimately defeat him once and for all at Calvary.

At the close of the age, we will be given wedding garments that are radiant, spotless and without blemish and here is a definite picture of wedding garments covered in a bright array of jewels. This is a beautiful bride, extravagantly decked out in the best her bridegroom can afford to give her. And that is everything of His best, for the bride He has always loved so much, has travelled the infinitely long journey from heaven to earth to give and to sacrifice everything He has for her.

POTHOLES 'SHORT THOUGHTS'

HEART OF A LIONESS

The pride of lion was stalking a group Oryx, a beautiful species of African antelope. One female had just given birth and when the chase erupted, she fled. As often happens in the savage cruelty of life on the African plains, she tripped and fell, making her an easy target for the hunters and leaving the newly born calf orphaned and all alone.

Then something unusual happened. The little orphan, having not yet learned what enemies were about, approached one of the lionesses without any natural fear, causing complete confusion in the predator. Without succour from a proper mother, there was no hope for the orphaned Oryx and for a week the two highly unlikely companions lived side by side in this aberrational relationship, one unable to feed, the other unable to hunt.

Why did the lioness not attack? Experts say that her hunting instincts are triggered by animals fleeing and because this one did not flee she had no idea what to do about it.

Meeting lions in the wild is terrifying. Ask anyone whose spent time in the wild! The bible tells us that 'Satan is like a roaring lion looking for someone to devour' (1 Peter 5: 8) and that makes him look equally terrifying (Colossians 2: 15). Yet Jesus encourages us to 'face the roar and overcome' as He has given us all the armour we need for protection (see Ephesians chapter 6). When we do this we find that although he is an enemy, all he is really is just a roar. Jesus disarmed him and made a spectacle of him at the cross. There are no teeth or claws.

On the other hand, all the spiritual armour we have only protects our front. If we turn our back to run away from the enemy we make ourselves vulnerable and wide open to attack.

Keep on facing the enemy. There is no other way. If you are afraid, ask Jesus for mastery over that fear; remembering that no matter what happens we are destined to win.

MEMORY VERSES:—
1 Peter 5: 8
. . . Be sober; be vigilant; because your adversary the devil walks about like a roaring lion, seeking whom he may devour

Colossians 2: 15
. . . Having disarmed principalities and powers, He made a public spectacle of them, triumphing over them in it.

WHEN WE ARE IN CHRIST, WE ARE RULING AND REIGNING
IN RIGHTEOUSNESS AND PEACE WITH HIM
IN THE HEAVENLIES OVER THE DEVIL AND
HIS PRINCIPALITIES AND POWERS

POTHOLES 'SHORT THOUGHTS

EVERYTHING WE NEED

God spoke and all creation came into being. We can only ponder of the depth of the raw grinding power of just His spoken word; as everything from the tiniest single-cell creatures to whole galaxies owe their existence; their very lives to that powerful word. Genesis 1 presents us with this cosmic view of creation and Genesis 2 'fine tunes' it with a focus given specifically to the humans made in God's image.

And then we wonder why it all went so terribly wrong, if this source of power in which it all has its origins is so infinite. How many times have you thought through all these aspects of our origins, the beauty of creation and then the tragedy of the Fall? About what has been revealed to us, and more specifically, what has not.

When God created us, He favoured us above all other creatures, for we alone were made in His image, a little lower than angels. He made marriage and the family which also was meant to be an earthly representation of the continual expressions of agape (unconditional) love that flows between the three members of the Godhead; Father, Son and Holy Spirit. He breathed His own life into our nostrils, thereby making us immortal. He had a right to expect singular service from so favoured a being; that He may have been able to say about us the same things He said about Jesus: *This is My beloved Son, in whom I am well pleased.*

We could have enjoyed a close family relationship with Him, but we jerked free of His care and lost everything, just as He knew we would and He made provision for that before the earth even came into existence. The bible, from start to finish, is a love story of God who will do everything, and stop at nothing, to bring home to Himself the people He loves so much.

He gave us His only begotten Son, Jesus. He came to restore all that was lost. Everything He accomplished, He did as both man and God; a man totally dependent on the power of God. In doing so, He has given us His fullness, because He understands everything we go through. And it is in His fullness we find everything that we need.

He can meet us at every single point of need. And that is about as perfect as everything can get. He fills the emptiness, feeds the hunger, slakes the thirst and brings healing to those who keep looking intently up to Him. He restores broken relationships. His power sets us free from fear, shame and crushing sin. All these and a myriad of other aspects of life that come at some time to every human life, bringing home the truth that an UNFALLEN WORLD COULD NEVER, EVER HAVE GLORIFIED GOD THE WAY JESUS CHRIST HIS SON HAS DONE.

The angels in heaven know God as Creator and they get along fine with that. But since we have fallen, and especially since Jesus' life on earth, we have come to know many more facets to this divine character. Jesus has now come as our Messiah, our Saviour and Redeemer: all titles we can know intimately and rely upon and praise in good times as well as difficult ones, but angels can only marvel at from a distance.

Despite everything, the shame and tragedy of the Fall, God still works all things together for His glory and the good of those called according to His purposes.

MEMORY VERSE
Colossians 2: 9
'. . . *For in Him dwells all the fullness of the Godhead bodily; and you are complete in Him, who is the head of all principality and power.*'

YOU LIVE IN JESUS CHRIST, JESUS CHRIST LIVES IN YOU
HERE IS THE POWER TO SET YOU FREE TO
LIVE AND REIGN IN LIFE

POTHOLES 'JOYBAG'

LETTERS FROM A BOARDING SCHOOL

Dear Dad and Mom,

Whoopah! Here I am, finally settled into boarding school and making a difference to this weird breed of kids I'd call 'townies'. We have loads of lessons, and being in a co-ed school is a bit different. It takes some getting used to!

The townies grumble about the early start, but after living on a dairy farm all my life, and getting up at 4.30 a.m. every morning often in the freezing cold, damp rain or snow of a midwinter's morning, I tend to think of this a more of a long, long lie-in, and it's a seriously easy way to start the school day.

At home we always milked all the cows before we had anything to eat, but here we have breakfast in a big dining room before lessons even start. Each table has a head pupil, and it is his job to make sure we finish all our food. Weird idea! Of course I finish all my food. Some of the townies don't finish their food and they sneak what's left over to me. No wonder they sometimes fall asleep during lessons and don't do well on the sports field.

The morning is mostly taken up with lessons, and in the afternoon we get to play some sport, which I like the best, being strong and healthy from all that farm life! I'm trying very hard at my lessons. Even the teachers say I'm trying. My Geography teacher thinks I could get lost in my own backyard. I told him I can roam around the farm all by myself and still make it back to the house. He said, 'I don't believe you' so I invited him round some time to see for himself. He smiled happily. I think he likes the idea.

The English teacher says I have a remarkable ability to tell astounding stories. Apparently the Religious Instruction teacher told her I said I knew why David had picked up five smooth pebbles when he only really needed one to kill the big giant, Goliath. I said he'd got the other five because he knew that he was gonna get heck from *Mrs* Goliath and all their kids when she found out. The English teacher thinks I should become a lawyer or a reporter or something like that. This is very great praise from such a good teacher. I tell her that all I really want to do is work on the farm and she said, 'That's impressive!' So I know we are getting on really well.

I don't get on the with Algebra teacher at all, sadly. I asked him one day to please stop making me look for his ex because I don't think she's coming back. He was very unhappy about that. He told me I wasn't making any effort at all. In fact, I conclude that if it wriggles it's Biology and if it stinks it's Chemistry and if I can't do it, it's Maths.

The sports coach is the best. He sends us on these cross-country runs, which he says are quite long, and who am I to contradict him? The only problem is that he insists I wear my trainers. He's worried I might hurt my feet or something if I don't. As if! Some of the other kids can't quite make it, so they try and do anything they possibly can to shorten the run. I wonder why?

Some afternoons we do athletics and I enjoy the throwing exercises the most—javelin, shot put and discus. The sports coach says we have to throw as far as we can, but he told me I mustn't throw the javelin at any teachers who happen to be passing by. All I did was lose my balance—I swear!

We also do archery and I like this kind of target practice. It's so much easier to hit a standing target than a running one, especially one with that great big black bull's eye in the middle. Who can possibly miss it? After learning to hit moving targets like pheasants this is really easy.

I've had a few problems with bullies. Well, not me exactly, but one of the girls who is quite small and shy (Alice is her name) was being bullied by a group of rough girls and boys—about five of them in all. I took them on behind the toilets and gave them a beating and such what for they'll never forget. It was epic triumph of note! Since then, the bullies keep away from her, and I keep an eye on things.

We have swimming lessons once a week at the local sports club and guess what? The pool is heated! It's more like swimming in a bathtub except the chemicals smell gross, but at least I can see the bottom. Also the changing rooms are way too hot, which is a pity. I get claustrophobic in there, and nearly ran out without my clothes on. We swim a lot of lengths—much more than I could swim in the cold dam at home.

I guess the lessons are the hard part, for me anyway. Alice helps me with my Math's. That's her way of saying thanks. She's really clever and makes it all sound so easy and she's a good friend to have.

Anyway, best of parents, tell my brothers that when it's their turn to come here, they'll find it all epic Whoopah! Just like I did.

Your loving daughter,
Mary Jane

CHAPTER FOUR

THE DAYS OF GRAIN, NEW WINE AND OIL

PART TWO

'Andy Shaw is missing,' Charlie Canning told us one Saturday when we'd gathered for a concert. In those days Missing Persons was an extremely rare event in Zimbabwe.

'Any details?' we asked clamouring around him, concerned and serious before bringing the matter to prayer.

'He went to Cleveland Dam yesterday afternoon to be alone and to pray. He didn't return home. Pat, his wife, is really worried.' Cleveland Dam was a small dam on the outskirts of Harare. It was surrounded by rocky outcrops which made a great playground for group picnics and was usually quite popular any time of the year.

They'd gone to Cleveland Dam to look but there was no sign of either Andy or the car he'd been using, a Toyota Cressida belonging to his father-in-law.

I'd met Andy years before through his sister, Alison Shaw, and we'd been blessed to have him minister to us at Highlands Presby as the Youth Pastor on Sunday evenings before he'd left to start his own church. I telephoned Alison that night to give her moral support. We knew what it was like to have someone go missing and have no clue as to either their whereabouts or even whether they were still alive.

When Charlie informed us of his disappearance, it was already nearly 24 hours later. Anything could have happened in that time. Immediately we began praying, but we knew there was a chance it was already too late. By the time Pat realized her husband was missing, it might have been too late. The sickening, sinking feeling threatened to overwhelm any hope that there was still a slight chance he was alive and well somewhere, just not where he should have been. I tried to jam down the painful lump in my throat. Pointless grieving until we knew for sure.

Andy's disappearance made the news headlines that night and everywhere posters with the words 'IMPORTANT NOTICE: MISSING' across the top and a great photo of Andy underneath went up everywhere. Interest spread rapidly until it literally became nationwide. Although Cleveland Dam was the obvious place to start, Andy's disappearance triggered a massive search. Everywhere churches, farmers, ordinary townsfolk, police, and concerned people got involved in the search and spreading the word, combing the countryside, probing, asking questions and praying.

Andy's and Pat's fathers got together to organize a large sum of money as a reward for information regarding his whereabouts. And another player came onto the field who would become highly significant in solving the case. He was a young African Police officer who had fought in the war alongside Andy and they'd got to know each other well. During that time he'd come to hold Andy in very high esteem and he was the one who warned the family that if Andy's disappearance was linked to some crime, then the perpetrators of that crime would try to claim the reward whether Andy was alive or not. So the phone lines were tapped and the Police were listening in on all the calls. One day the call they were waiting for came in.

'We have Andrew and we'll give him back in return for the money,' and anonymous caller informed them. So the negotiations began.

'Is Andy still alive?' they asked him.

The caller reassured them that Andy was indeed alive, but he wanted the money before he agreed to restore Andy to his family. The two fathers, very courageously, insisted that it be an exchange—the money for Andy at the same time. They wanted to know for sure that he was still alive. As they kept the stranger talking for as long as possible, then came the vital clue the quietly listening Policeman was waiting for—the evidence that would tell him where the call was being made from. In the background came the sound of an ambulance siren wailing.

Immediately the Police telephoned the hospitals in Harare to find out who had dispatched an ambulance and where it was heading. Pararenyatwa Hospital had dispatched an ambulance to a shopping centre in one of the local African townships. The Police sent in a SWAT team, simply rounded up and arrested everyone in the shopping centre, before questioning them systematically until they got hold of the ones they were looking for. In the end they found three out of a group of four African men who were responsible for Andy's disappearance.

The next day the old posters were replaced with a new one: 'IMPORTANT NOTICE: FOUND' together with the same picture of Andy, handsome young and smiling appeared and the story unfolded. Andy had been alone and praying at Cleveland Dam when this group of men approached him. Initially there was no conflict and there was evidence that Andy had even greeted them. The details were unclear but from there something went wrong, Andy was attacked and murdered. His body was dumped in a shallow grave at Cleveland Dam and the car was stolen. With the major national publicity in the case, however, the car became too hot to handle and so that was relegated to the earth as well.

By the time Andy's body was found, he was too badly decomposed to recognize immediately without proper forensic testing. But his wedding ring and his watch were still on the body, as well as the shirt he'd been wearing. Also Andy had very small hands and feet for a man (a Shaw trait, Alison told me) so Pat had enough to go on to make a positive identification.

Capital Punishment was still law in Zimbabwe at that time, so the three were tried, sentenced to death and put on Death Row where one later committed suicide. Pat, very courageously, visited them and gave them bibles and told them she had forgiven them. My heart ached for them all; Pat and their two children who were still very young, but mainly for Alison, his sister and my friend.

Andy's funeral was held in the big building of the Northside Community Church which holds around 1 000 people in its auditorium. About 1 400 people came as a show of solidarity and many had to stand outside. Andy left an amazing legacy of love and strength and we, who were left to carry on, could only emulate him as we had seen him emulate Jesus Christ. That legacy will live on in his life and ministry, his family, the songs he wrote and the Church he established.

A few days later, a group of us went with 'Yadah' up to Nyanga for another concert. In the cool green and fragrant garden where we stayed, I took time out to sit alone amongst the colourful flowers and sniffing the warming air laden with the exotic scent of jasmine, heady with the onset of spring. On the hillsides, the msasa trees, with their early spring leaves coloured the scene like liquid fire pouring down into the valleys. The orchard trees were smothered with pink-and-white blooms which would produce apples and pears in autumn. What a lovely setting to grieve in.

Andy would have been delighted to see the turnout and more importantly, the unity at his thanksgiving service. These were the things he'd worked so hard and fought so long for. And now he was no longer with us—gone suddenly before any of us—even his wife knew there was a problem. Instead of being a burning, vital flame in the midst of us, he was at home in the immediate presence of Jesus Christ and enjoying the fruits of his faith which he had whilst on earth. How on earth did you do without someone like Andy Shaw? The world so badly needs people like him.

It was one of those moments when the Lord ministered directly and gently spoke to me about each one of us being a flame and passing that flame onto others. Andy had been such a flame, but he had passed that onto others who would, in turn, burn brightly for Jesus Christ. That way, Andy's work and his legacy would live on.

As I sat there, a 'gogomannekie' appeared in the undergrowth and climbed part way up the trunk of a gnarled old msasa tree. He was watching me on one side, and as I had his full attention, I leaned over and eased my left hand around the other side, giving him a fright and poor creature leapt up and shot off to find a safer haven. I left the garden smiling. 'Gogomannekies' make excellent pets, I'm told. But I prefer to see them ranging in freedom where I can enjoy the occasional sight of one doing its own thing in peace.

Some months later when Pat, newly widowed, went to a Church service where a well-known South African minister (who had a powerful prophetic ministry) was taking a service the Lord gave a special message to her. Towards the end of the service, the minister said to her, 'I don't know who you are, but you are being guarded by two the hugest angels I have ever seen!' We were thankful that through all the grief and trauma of losing a much-loved husband and being on her own to bring up two young children; Pat had been given also a wonderful heavenly tribute. The veil between that which is unseen and the realm in which we live here on earth was lifted for that precious glimpse by someone capable and responsible enough to do the right thing with it. Praise God for His endless blessings but especially the ones we cannot see.

Having a ministry in helping people getting to know Jesus in a vital and real way was so exciting and fulfilling and that was one way of passing on the living, vital flame. It could also be heartbreaking, even traumatic as we uncovered pain and problems we never knew existed. Ministering to teenagers as we did, I thought most of the problems we'd come across were the usual generational gap problems with parents, peer pressure, dented self-image. Over the 1980's decade we'd had the additional challenge of helping black and white Zimbabweans integrate in a more vital, powerful way with the most pressing purpose being rebuilding the country's economy which had been sapped during the war years. The white population dropped to around 80 000, but the African population, with better health, education, employment and such began increasing.

In the ministry, none of us were prepared for the horrors and heartache that we did come across; horrors and heartache that youngsters rarely talk about willingly. Sometimes the silence is due to fear of ostracism or ridicule and the need for acceptance beats hard in the heart of youngsters. Silence could also be a result of threats, guilt and shame. But the price of silence and bearing the burden alone is always too high.

Back in Zimbabwe in the 1990's the teen suicide rate amounted to around 100 documented suicides per year. There were always going to be that portion which could not be verified as suicides and it might have given the families concerned more comfort to have them ruled as 'accidental' deaths or deaths by misadventure. One hundred may not sound like much, given the African population of around 6 million and the white around 80 000, but it is still 100 too many. The heartbreak became all too real for us when a young friend from school days committed suicide around that time.

What could possibly cause such a young person to want to end their life? If some of the problems that were shared with us, some of the stories that we prayed over are anything to go by, it is hardly surprising. The 'usual' problems of teenage years came up certainly and I don't want to belittle these problems in any way. Being trapped by peer pressure, difficult home relationships, and the myriad other things that can cause low self-image in a young person are all serious and need to be treated as such. For young people, trying to cope with puberty, the pressure of exams, new relationships and trying to decide what future career appeals and what you want to train for is enormous pressure at a time in life where most people have yet to develop the coping skills necessary to deal with it. But there were others too. A huge number of youngsters admitted to being abused either physically or sexually by an adult they knew and should have been able to trust. 'Yadah' wrote a song entitled *The One Who Touches You* in response to their heart cries and whenever they played it, yet more youngsters would speak about the abuse they'd suffered, often for the first time ever.

Irresponsible drinking and drug-taking by parents and their friends also came up far too often. Several members of our counselling team itself had been sexually abused, one had been raped, and others had had problems with drugs or alcohol. All had an opportunity to bring them to Jesus and show others how to do the same thing.

What could we leave them with, in the very short space of time we had to minister to them? Usually we had around an hour, but sometimes it was less. There wasn't any one thing we could do or say to give them any real help, but we could introduce them to the One who could make a difference—Jesus Christ. We often thought of ourselves as people who are 'standing in the gap'—it is as though we had Jesus by one hand and the broken-hearted youngster by the other—and all we had to do was introduce them to one another, joining their hands together and moving our own out of the way. There isn't any circumstance in life that Jesus cannot heal and repair, working all things together for our good and for His glory.

'My Dad abused both my sister and myself. She contracted Chlamydia and that destroyed her fertility.' How does a woman whose been through such an ordeal ever heal sufficiently enough to be able to love men? What happens if she marries but can't have children?

As counsellors, we learned that it was very unwise to ever say to someone, 'I understand,' when we had no experience of what they had been through. Even if you did, you still had to be wary of saying, 'I understand,' because we react to life's circumstances in different ways. One of the ways God helped us to minister was to give us supernatural insight into someone's problem.

I remember the first time such insight occurred. I was with Elizabeth and we were sitting on a bench in the lush green grounds of the National Botanical Gardens in Harare. It was a beautiful day and the hot sun shone on the bright waters of the lake, surrounded by the lush greenery of numerous different plants and trees. Suddenly the colours faded and everything went into varying shades of grey as the Lord showed me right into the pain in her heart. Then I was able to pray more effectively for her.

There was a time, when praying for a barren couple (who'd been married ten years and remained childless), I saw her with what looked like a basketful of fruit in her abdomen. Delightful picture that it was; it took several seconds for me to figure out that the Lord was telling me her womb would be fruitful. Another couple verified the vision and eighteen months later she fell pregnant. They now have two beautiful boys.

We also learned that it is unwise to ever tell anyone exactly what to do unless you are 100% sure that is God's will. Usually, however, it is God's way to direct a person's heart the way He wants it to go and allow the person to discover all He wants to teach them. If you 'got ahead' of God, He may well arrange the same set of circumstances to come around again, allowing the person time and space to learn the lesson. Often it's better to help them see ahead to potential consequences of their actions instead.

The biggest problem with youngsters was the same obsession with the idea of marriage. Some of them, you just couldn't get their sights off some priceless romance they kept imagining. As a divorcee, I had to be careful not to allow my own bitter experiences put a dent in any young person's high ideals. But I do believe that sometimes the only way the Lord can really convince us that we don't need something, and that is to allow us to have it. Parents of young children know how often that particular lesson is true.

This approach is, of course, limited when ministering to someone with alcohol or drug addiction. They usually need both higher support and higher structure and tougher love. They were often the ones with a very low self-esteem, often a total inability to accept what Jesus came to offer and extreme difficulty in breaking free from the damaging behavioural pattern. Usually, this type of obsessive-compulsive behaviour needs deliverance. Then it needs a whole new structured support in changing the habits that allowed the person to become addicted in the first place. Trying to convince such a person that Jesus Christ does truly love them could be incredibly difficult. But once they'd got hold of that truth, a whole new person often emerged.

During this time, we became increasingly aware of the significance of the New Testament covenant of grace, Jesus' shockingly personal and intimate interest in our lives. We all need to have a good understanding of that amazing grace; it's empowering and radically life-changing effects. This love for all people, all sinners and it didn't matter how badly we had lived; we could never, ever get beyond the reach of that grace. Oh wow! How often a person admitted to being the one responsible for destroying their own life—or even the lives of others—and feeling that Jesus could not possibly ever love them or want to get to know them. The joy of seeing them coming to a whole new understanding of what it truly was Jesus came to offer.

The dying thief on cross who could only say: *Remember me when you come into your throne* was NEVER going to have the opportunity to do anything right, or make restitution, or pray or tithe or *anything* to earn salvation and yet Jesus still said to him: *Truly I say to you, tonight you will be with Me in paradise*, that thief a kind of firstfruits of the rest of us who would later on accept all that He came to offer.

I still find awesome power in the scene of Simon's dinner party in Luke chapter 7 where Jesus got into trouble for just one person, a *woman* and a *prostitute* at that. No, I am the one who puts shameful and disgusting labels on her life. He didn't. As a direct result, she was restored to her community, but He continued to be in trouble! No use trying to explain God who will not be entirely contained by our words.

We do all we can, and words do carry power to change people's lives; faith does come by hearing. And to see someone's eyes suddenly light up with the realisation that they are loved by God after all is just superb.

When a broken-hearted person looks up at you with the light of new hope in their eyes and asks the question, "Is restoration possible? Can my life really be made worthwhile?" And that deepest heart cry of all, "Can Jesus really love *me still?*" Of course He can because His love is never based on what you do. What a priceless gift we have to give in those words. But they are only our words, and we rely on the mighty power of Jesus to imbibe them with His eternal life. A life is changed, hope is given and I pray that for many it would be a turning point, a brand new start.

Even knowing the theory, we almost missed this until God (I'm sure) led Jack to our group. Jack was in his early thirties, with a naughty face, curly brown hair and a cheeky glint in his very blue eyes. He also had a ready smile, but just his looks alone made me believe every word he spoke when he described some of his spurious adventures with our group. Then he would share some amazingly deep insights into the gospel and I never knew quite what to make of him. He'd been 'disciplined' by the established Church (I have no idea what specifically for, but it wasn't hard to believe) and yet there was no doubt he also had a heart for God.

Every time he recounted some hellacious experience about drugs or alcohol, he certainly captured everyone's attention. But when he shared gospel truths, there was no apparent reaction from anyone at all. Things took a turn for the worse when some of the younger members of the team began complaining about Jack. They wanted him to be asked to leave—the drunken and drugged capers were getting them down. And yet, if we were supposed to be a counselling team, then it was people like Jack we were training to rescue. I couldn't allow anyone to leave, but how to address the problem? Chris Saint, Chris Parry and I thrashed it through.

'Trouble is, everyone's reacting to his hairy stories and ignoring the best part of him,' Chris Parry told me. 'We are, in fact, going about it in the wrong way. We're giving him negative reinforcement.'

'What can we do to change that?' I asked, really perplexed because I sensed we'd reached a 'watershed' experience. If we took the wrong turning, things would never be quite right again.

'We need to positively reinforce him, but without him realizing what we are doing,' Chris Saint said.

So we made a plan. We told everyone the same thing: 'When Jack talks about his riotous capers, ignore him and when he speaks about the gospel, then give him positive reinforcement by asking questions or making comments, any kind of feedback you can think of but don't let on we're doing this because it's bound to come across as phony if he finds out.' From that Monday evening onwards, something changed for the better. I'm no expert but I do believe such decisions change something in the unseen realms.

Jack began to change almost imperceptibly. He told us other hair-raising stories, about how he went right into the way-out gwandashas, a white man on his own spreading the gospel to the African people who were poor and very isolated. He had little money, very little help and almost inevitably became seriously ill with malaria.

Whilst trying to hitch a lift home to get the medical treatment he needed, Jack collapsed on the roadside. Hovering between life and death, he spoke directly to what appeared to be a heavenly being, 'If God allows me to live, I will serve Him all the days of my life,' Jack told him. And shortly afterwards he was rescued by a passing motorist and taken to hospital where convalescence was swift. But, like most people who make such promises in dire circumstances, Jack did not have the courage or the strength to keep his side of the bargain and having been disciplined by a Church, decided to try a Christian group outside of Church and so he came to us.

As the weeks went by, we began to see a better side of Jack and with positive reinforcement so that side grew. It was almost as if we were building him a bigger frame and he was growing to fill it. The change was remarkable, and powerful.

Having reached a higher level of understanding, we could all then appreciate what a courageous man he really was; going into isolated and remote places often alone and unsupported with minimal resources to bring Jesus to some of the poorest people in Zimbabwe. I could imagine him sleeping on a cold, hard floor inside a mud hut with thatched roof. There probably would have been a smoky cooking fire in the middle, and everything would have absorbed the acrid smell of wood smoke. Maybe he would have had a little sadza and relish for a meal, and water to drink from the nearest river or stream. Silver and gold I didn't have, Jack, but if I could do it all again, I'd give you more support and prayer cover. You were a true brother in Christ, deeply, painfully honest about your shortcomings. You made yourself so very vulnerable to a group of people who initially, at least didn't understand either you or the enormity of the drama that was unfolding.

Some years later, after the group had disbanded and Jack had left for England, he wrote me a letter. 'I love you, he wrote, not in a romantic sense, but because you were the one person who believed in me, who trusted in me to find the strength to make a new start. Today I am a brand new man because I saw in you that Jesus really did care about someone like me.' Wow! Was that a lesson to move the even the strongest heart. One man in pain, given a new lease of life in His name! It reminds me of a saying I read once: *Jesus said, 'I will make you fishers of men.' We catch them—He'll clean them!* That's grace and morality in their correct order. Catch them as they are and bring them to Him and let Him do the rest! We can't force people to live up to a standard that we ourselves are incapable of achieving before we think they are good enough to be accepted.

Something similar happened years later, also at a bible study when I prayed for someone who seemed to have ties holding her back. One day Chloe sat in the group and simply poured out the pain she felt she had brought on her own head. She had become dangerously addicted to over-the-counter painkillers which contained codeine and paracetamol. Codeine can be addictive, but it is not the only problem with overdoing painkillers. Our liver can only break down paracetamol at a certain rate and to take more than the recommended dose, especially on a continual level for months is to risk liver failure and that is a horrible way to die. To make matters more complicated, Chloe also fell pregnant unexpectedly in the middle of all this.

For days I could not believe the enormity of what had happened. Right in our midst, our good way of life, our weekly bible study and garden club meetings, without any of us realizing it but something had gone horribly wrong for someone. We prayed for release from the addiction. We prayed that Almighty God in His infinite mercy would cleanse both Chloe's system and that of her unborn child, removing all the toxins from the drugs. Today, nearly nine years on, both are well; the young boy and his Mum. They're living in Australia and the other side of the world from us. I miss them so much. But I'm also very thankful for the grace which set Chloe free from the addiction and she could enjoy her children growing up.

And so, for people whose lives had been blighted by wrong choices, there was still every opportunity for a brand new start. But it is one that revolves around grace—not to be confused with morality. The Kingdom of God rejoices every time a sinner comes into that kingdom—but it's a 'Come As You Are' party. It's about a relationship with the eternal Creator and Redeemer. It has nothing to do with a set of rules. So do yourself a favour and don't let anyone ever tell you otherwise.

POTHOLES 'BELOW THE SURFACE'

'MIND THE GAP'

I'm sure you've all heard many times the one question Evangelists really like to ask. 'If you were to die tonight, and God were to ask you why you should be allowed into heaven, what would your answer be?' And they wait for people to reply with the usual me-centred answers, like, 'I worked hard, I looked after my family and my ageing parents. I never robbed anybody or murdered anybody and I only told a few white lies when it was necessary.'

We humans tend to grade sin and wrongdoing from minor infractions like breaking the rules of the road or little white lies. We wouldn't, for a minute, think a jail sentence necessary for such things. We leave that to the much more serious crimes like murder, armed robbery, child abuse and quite rightly so.

I couldn't help feeling so sad yesterday, when I heard on the news that after 40 years the Police have finally decided to call off the search for the body of the last Moors murder victim. If Ian Brady knows where the body is, he's not saying. He's destroyed not only that child's life, but the lives of his family as well.

But our laws are not the same as God's Law and actually, God doesn't grade sin at all. To Him sin is sin, and even if you have one or two small sins in your life you are not justified in entering heaven. Your good deeds will not outweigh the bad ones.

Salvation, from start to finish is a work of Jesus Christ. He came to fulfil the Old Testament Law and usher in the New Testament Covenant of GRACE. And we talk about GRACE as being 'God's Riches At Christ's expense.'

And Grace is what justifies us before a holy God. There's an easy way to remember justification, it basically means 'Just As If I'd Never Sinned.'

So it's really, really important to understand the difference between the two covenants because this was the issue that separated the Early Church from the Jewish community as a whole, and the reason why Jews persecuted the early Christians. Today, Jews who have become Christians are often referred to as 'Messianic Jews' so that there is a differentiation. The Old Testament Covenant of the Law was only ever given to Israel, and it was only ever given for a limited time period. If we could have been saved through the Law, then Moses would have been our Saviour. All the Law can really do is point out the fact that we are sinners, but it cannot save us.

One of the reasons why reading the four gospels can be difficult is because although Jesus came to bring in the new Covenant of Grace, He still lived under the Law. He never broke God's given Law. Many, many of the parables point to Grace and tell us that all we have to do to receive eternal life is nothing except to believe in Jesus Christ.

Paul, being a Pharisee of the Pharisees and a highly intelligent man was the one who understood the difference between the two covenants and his writings reflect that. The book of Romans has a great deal of detail regarding grace, whilst Galatians deals with the dangers of mixing the two covenants. The book of Hebrews refers to the Mosaic Law as 'the shadow', and refers to grace 'the substance' and compares the two covenants.

The verse we have here is one of the highlight verses of the New Testament. Paul had been through this amazing experience of being transported to the third heaven and despite his heavenly experiences, he apparently had not found the answer to his torment. In all his writings, Paul very rarely lets us into his deep heart, into the place where he feels pain. This is one of the rare occasions of insight into his despair. Feel his despair as three times he pleads with the Lord to take away his thorn in the flesh and three times the Lord answered him with these immortal words:

My grace is sufficient for you
My strength is made perfect in weakness.

Sometimes people might be tempted to think that this is an example of unanswered prayer, but it isn't really. God was simply telling him, 'You have the answers inside you already, because you understand Grace.' The exciting thing about grace is that not only does it bring salvation but also grace EMPOWERS us to live above the circumstances of life. Grace empowers us to stand in the face of our enemy who would destroy us.

- Grace takes us through the hard times, empowering us to take control of our lives rather than be overwhelmed by circumstances.
- We no longer have to be controlled by unwanted thought patterns and peculiar behaviour because grace empowers us to be holy.

And yes, there will always be a gap between where we are in holiness, and the ultimate standard of holiness that God demands. When you use the tube or train services around London, as the doors open, you often here a voice over the loudspeaker reminding you to 'Mind The Gap'. We know we cannot be perfectly holy, so we are always mindful of that gap, and wary of the consequences. But always remembering, always bearing in mind that God knows and understands that gap and that's one of the provisions of His grace. Grace, amazing grace, closes the gap.

- Grace brings empowering love that makes a difference in other people's lives.
- Grace enables us to share these life-changing truths.
- One day God will show us off as trophies of His grace to our one true enemy, the devil.

I've been writing a study from the book of Joshua about the prostitute Rahab, who hid the Israelite spies at great personal danger. In return she and her family were saved, and she became part of the Messianic line, which might seem a strange thing for God to do with a prostitute. Because of that, people sometimes attempt to sanitize her and say maybe she was an innkeeper. The bible is quite clear about what she was—and so should we. She was a prostitute who became a trophy of God's grace.

No matter what we have done, no matter what the depths of our despair, or what life has held for us or maybe more to the point, what it didn't hold for us, we too, are trophies of God's grace.

And finally to go back to our original question which we think God might ask, 'Why should I let you into My heaven?' To be honest, I don't think He would ask that question at all. The only one He will ask, if any, is: 'What did you do with My Son?' The only answer He needs is, 'By grace, I believe in Jesus Christ and what He did to set me free.'

POTHOLES 'SHORT THOUGHTS'

PRINCE OF PEACE

In John 14: 27 Jesus promised His disciples: *'Peace I leave with you, My peace I give you; not as the world gives do I give you. Let not your heart be troubled neither let it be afraid.'*

Worldly peace is but a mere shadow of its deeply abiding, empowering heavenly counterpart. Before we come to faith in Jesus we are enemies with God and there is no heavenly peace. Today it's so easy for those of us who would have been classified as Gentiles to forget just how far off we were and what a blessing it is to have this covenant extended to us that we might also be part of God's eternal family.

In Romans 5, Paul develops the theme further by explaining that *'therefore being justified by faith we have peace with God through our Lord Jesus Christ'* because there is a divine exchange that is made. God took all of our sins and placed them on Jesus who knew no sin so that He could be sin in our place. But that was only the first half of this divine exchange. The second half was that God placed the righteousness of Jesus into our heavenly account and all we have to do to receive this righteousness is to believe! This grace is 'God at Work' and we rest upon this finished work. And yet this is only the start of this gracious gift which is multi-facetted. It is peace with God.

Peace of God is the depths of peace which permeate our beings so that we find no matter what life's experiences might be we will still experience deep, unshakeable peace. Despite the terrible storm, Jesus was asleep in the bottom of the boat. The stronger our faith is, the greater our peace will be and fear will not override it. It comes with knowing that every circumstance we face has already passed through the sovereign hands of a capable and loving God and that He has already dealt with it all before the foundation of the world.

Jesus is the Prince of Peace and if He abides in you by faith, then allow Him to fill you with such peace that no circumstance of life will ever shake you. Peace is also a fruit of the Holy Spirit. State your position in Christ out loud, and He will place at your disposal all of heaven's resources. Then you can move forward with absolute reassurance that He is in control of any outcome.

There also biblical references to the spiritual warfare which we true believers wage against Satan; probably the most famous are Psalm 91, 'The prayer of perfect protection against all kinds of evil' and Ephesians chapter 6 which details the spiritual weapons we're given for spiritual warfare. But one of the greatest spiritual weapons is peace that Paul refers to in Romans 16: 19, 20: *'For your obedience has become known to all. Therefore I am glad on your behalf; but I want you to be wise in what is good, and simple concerning evil. And the God of peace will crush Satan under your feet shortly. The grace of our Lord Jesus Christ be with you. Amen'* so when we abide in the peace of God we appropriate that peace as a weapon and God Himself will use our feet to crush Satan swiftly.

We rule and reign with Jesus in the heavenlies in righteousness and peace—no wonder the devil hates the gospel of peace. No wonder he is so afraid of committed Christians. Jesus shows us off to him as trophies of His grace. And when we rule and reign in life—then the devil certainly does not.

So often the enemy attacks are designed first of all to rob us of our peace—and no wonder! Stand firmly in your position in the Prince of Peace and through you He will destroy the enemy's power. Once again, Jesus would only do that by the power of His grace. He would never do that if we were still under Law and striving in our own strength, to overcome an enemy whose strength is superior to our own. However, his strength can never equal that of God. The created being can never equal or overcome the Great Uncreated, the Great I am in whose power and peace you rest!

MEMORY VERSE:—
John 14: 27
'. . . *"Peace I leave with you; My peace I give you; not as the world gives do I give you. Let not your heart be troubled, neither let it be afraid."'*

IF YOU WERE THE ONLY PERSON WHO EVER LIVED
JESUS WOULD STILL HAVE LOVED YOU ENOUGH
TO DIE FOR YOU,
SO LET HIS GOOD, GOOD GIFTS FLOOD YOUR LIFE
LIKE A RIVER AND KEEP YOU IN
PERFECT PEACE.

POTHOLES 'SHORT THOUGHTS'

'BUT . . . DO THIS FIRST.'

1 kings 17

Biblical narratives both plumb the depths and scale the heights of human experience. There really isn't anything in the complex tapestries of our own lives for which we cannot find a parallel somewhere in scripture. So many times, throughout the Old Testament, we find jewels of grace where, with no reference to the Law, the sacrificial system or following a set of rules, and even for people who are not Jews, God reaches out in powerful grace to radically change the hopelessness in someone's life.

For the widow of Zarepath, life and death were probably constant companions at the same table and it was all she could do to keep them apart until the long drought meant the real possibility of death finally overcoming. Her decision that day was based on it—to gather sticks, make one final meal for herself and her son, and succumb to the inevitable. People in the same heartbreaking situation today make that same decision.

Elijah did not try to change her mind; he simply subverted her plans for the day by saying, 'Do not fear, go and do as you have said, but make me a small cake from it first, and bring it to me.'

'But . . . do this first, and you will live.' In doing so, he pointed her thoughts in the direction of faith, hope and promise. 'But' is a small word that has that ability.

'But first,' he said to her, 'make this small change. Feed me, and then make something for you and your son.' It was a change of direction that did not even make sense for it required feeding him ahead of a very meagre meal. And he gave her two reassurances from Almighty God—*do not be afraid and there will be enough.*

As a result she took her eyes off that hopelessness and placed them firmly on what God could do through His servant and each day He provided them with enough oil and flour daily. That meant each day was still a test of faith, believing that God would again provide enough for the next day, and so they were fed by His sovereign hands for many days. It raises questions about life and death, relationships, communal sharing, whether there really is justice, our doubts and God's faithfulness.

How God handles the bread! How He handles the oil! What possibilities exist inside a change of direction and faith in what He can do! What an awesome God He is. Whatever your situation is today, give it all into the Hands of Infinite Possibilities, capable of giving all good gifts, and see what He can do with it.

MEMORY VERSE:
1 Kings 17: 24
Then the woman said to Elijah, 'Now by this I know that you are a man of God, and that the word of the Lord in your mouth is the truth.'

WHEN YOU READ THE SCRIPTURES LOOK FOR
TINY WORDS LIKE 'BUT' AND THE
HIGHLY SIGNIFICANT WAY THEY CHANGE
A SITUATION FROM DESPAIR TO
THE 'BUT' THAT BRINGS VIBRANT FAITH

POTHOLES 'JOY BAG'

THE RIGHT HEADING

There were only two aircraft leaving Maputo Airport in Mozambique that hot and still morning. Air Traffic Control had given them both their flight clearances with their individual departure headings. After the first aircraft had taken off, the second aircraft, with the First Officer at the controls, continued taxiing to the threshold.

'Look at that!' Dean, the First Officer, exclaimed to the Captain sitting on his left. 'They've taken off on our assigned heading! Idiots!' He continued to grumble as he approached the threshold. Seated next to him, the Captain sat silently as he watched his First officer manoeuvre the aircraft into position for take-off.

When they were ready to start rolling, the Captain turned to Dean and said, 'Which way are you going to go?'

'The same way they're going because they're on the heading ATC gave us.'

The Captain gave him a long, long stare and said to him, 'Did it not occur to you, even once, that you might then be the one on the wrong heading?' Their Dakota, being bigger and faster than the light aircraft ahead, would catch up.

Dean sat still, weighing up the possibilities. He could, of course, admit he was wrong and correct the heading he was on before risking a mid-air collision. Or he could be stubborn, wilful and carry on being wrong.

God has given us 'headings' for a life in Him and an instruction manual which covers everything we're likely to encounter. How often though, do we allow our pride or our own stubborn wilfulness to dictate a wrong heading? We end up on unnecessary collision courses. If we pursue those headings, they will lead to our ultimate ruin.

A common saying is that 'pride comes before a fall' but actually Proverbs goes one scarier when the writer states that *pride comes before destruction*' (see Proverbs 16: 18).

The only members of society Jesus continually confronted were the Pharisees—the religious leadership who would not believe they'd got everything wrong—and that thieves, prostitutes and other 'sinners' would go on through heaven's gates ahead of them. How many ever heeded the warning?

If we need some redirection, Jesus will tell us, either through His word, through other people who are wiser or through the still, small voice of the Holy Spirit. If He's talking to us about a wrong heading of one sort or another, then we should take heed of the warning and change. We will then arrive safely at our destination together.

Years ago, the Lockheed developed a very sophisticated spy plane called an SR-71 nicknamed 'Blackbird' capable of flying on the very edge of the earth's atmosphere. Operating at such high speeds at such high levels at that particular time in history, they could outrace or outpace any enemy action. Plus there were no ground-to-air missiles that could reach them whilst they were flying high above, and spying on, hostile countries below. If a surface-to-air missile launch was detected, they simply accelerated out of reach. Although a number of these aircraft crashed, not one was ever lost to enemy action.

Although the technical details are fascinating in their own right, I won't be able to describe them here, sadly. They do make fascinating reading, however. The one item, which interested me above all others, though, was the apparent presence somewhere in the flight deck of a placard carrying the words:—

> *Yea, though I travel through the valley of the shadow of death,*
> *I will fear no evil.*
> *For I am at 80 000 feet and climbing . . .*

And the same is for Christians everywhere! God has made us trophies of His magnificent grace through His Son Jesus Christ. He has lifted us up through the earthly and demonic realms, to be seated with Him in the heavenly realms.

YEA, THOUGH I WALK THROUGH THE VALLEY OF THE SHADOW OF DEATH, I WILL FEAR NO EVIL" PSALM 23

YOU KNOW YOU ARE OLD WHEN . . .

:D You remember when the Dead Sea was still alive . . .

:D You sink your teeth into a piece of steak—and they stay there . . .

:D The little old lady you help across the street is your wife . . .

:D Your secrets are safe with your friends because they can't remember them either . . .

:D Your children start looking middle-aged . . .

:D You and your teeth sleep in different places . . .

:D Your childhood toys are in a museum . . .

:D The candles on the cake cost more than the cake . . .

:D Your friends compliment you on your new crocodile-skin shoes—and you are barefoot . . .

:D You bore or frighten your grandchildren with stories of your youth when there was no TV, no video games, or computers. You drank straight out of the hosepipe, you shared drinking straws with your mates (and didn't get sick).

:D You rode a go-cart which didn't have any brakes . . .

:D You are abducted by aliens but then returned because they would prefer a live specimen . . .

:D You've given up wild oats for shredded wheat . . .

:D THE SENILITY PRAYER: 'God grant me the senility to forget the people I never liked anyway, the good fortune to run into the ones I do and the wisdom to know the difference.'

:D Finally:—

If you can't get rid of the skeletons in your closet
Then you might as well dress them up and
Make them dance!

CHAPTER FIVE

TUNUNU FARM

Dad retired from his job of airline pilot with an overseas flight in the Boeing 707 and finished with a spectacular low-level, high speed pass over the runway before his last landing as befits a Robin Hood who is a Senior Boeing Captain. No matter what you do, you really can't take the Robin Hood out of him! Retirement from the civilian airline, anyway; because despite the farming, the 'hangar doors' would open again into a whole new realm of flying that would take him back to his all-time favourite 'Iron Horse'—the Dakota. Dad became involved in a company called Tropic Air, Inter Air and Sky Relief at various times and spent 15 years flying for the ICRC (International Committee of the Red Cross) taking food aid and medical supplies into a number of the war-torn countries of Africa, often under difficult and dangerous conditions. It was, undoubtedly, the most challenging chapter in his entire flying career in many ways, although flying for the International Red Cross in war-torn countries usually involves oaths of secrecy.

When they began their new life on Tumbleweed Estates or 'Mukutu' farm shortly before the birth my own children, Kimberley, Robin and Timothy it was as if reliving the days of my own childhood, they were able to enjoy the benefits of the farm life, whilst living in the city. All regrets of selling 'Rippling Waters' were dispensed of shortly afterwards as it turned out to have an unexpected bonus.

The farm next door was managed by a young couple, Keith and Linda Marriott. A few years into the divorce, I met Linda's older brother Jim Tucker, who was managing farms in the Tengwe district further up the same main Harare-Kariba road. Jim, with his wide open and smiling face and strong and shapely 'rugby player's' legs was the one who really inspired happily romantic thoughts in me, although we built up a friendship over a period of four years first.

Before that happened, the wonderful joy of the Days of Grain, New Wine and Oil came to an end, where I lost almost everything and had to painfully rebuild my life yet again.

'Gran wants to sell her house,' Muz informed me one day. I was troubled. I couldn't afford to buy such a beautiful house in such a sought-after area. I had hoped to be rescued by some last-minute miracle of which I know the Lord is more than capable, but it was not to be.

By 1996/1997 the Zimbabwean economy was beginning to show signs of becoming insecure, although outwardly, they were hard to detect. New buildings were being erected everywhere and the roads were full of fancy vehicles. New shopping centres were blooming and I still think of the 1990's as the best decade in the country's history. For a year, I managed to rent a very expensive house, but rent prices were increasing and I had to accept that there was no way I could afford a home big enough for four of us.

Nothing can break a mother in two like having to accept the fact that she cannot financially afford to keep her children, and it was with a broken heart that I accepted the fact that they had to return to their father to live. He'd remarried by then and had had another child. Only my friend Elizabeth was in the same predicament and that year, she kept me sane. 'Yadah's' ministry had come to a close and I found myself in a digs with two single women. I tried to accept the lawyer's words that it would be wiser to allow the children to live where they were financially better off. Depriving them of everything they needed for proper development just so that I could hang onto them would only prove detrimental in the long run. Thankfully, we had the farm to go to over weekends.

Keeping despair at bay became increasingly difficult. One night I was woken by severe abdominal pain and I knew something was seriously wrong, but weeks of tests failed to reveal the cause and by then I was seriously ill. My throat was aflame and courses of antibiotics failed to cure the infection. One particular night I sought refuge on the cold green tiled bathroom floor and actually found relief from the raging fever by wrapping myself around the equally cold white porcelain toilet. When you can do something like that, and find relief, you know you are seriously ill.

Towards Easter time, the surgeon made a decision. 'We'll book you into the Avenues Clinic for a laparoscopy and when I can see what's wrong with you, I will continue with further surgery. Pointless bringing you round to tell you what's wrong with you before putting you under to operate again. I'll book you in after Easter. You don't want to be in hospital over Easter.'

'That will be too late. I don't think I can survive that long,' I told him and he took me seriously, thankfully. Two days later I signed a hospital form which stated, 'Laparoscopy . . . . Procedure?' Have you ever had to sign a medical form with the words 'Procedure' followed by a question mark and wondered what on earth you would be allowing them to do to you whilst you are anaesthetized and incapable of any action whatsoever?

Lying on the operating table as they prepped me for surgery was a huge test of faith. When I came round from surgery, drugged and confused, the abdominal pain was excruciating. A nurse came to speak to me and I asked her, 'When are they going to operate? I am in agony!' She smiled, told me not to worry and held my hand in her large and comforting one, whilst someone gave me morphine and the pain miraculously disappeared.

It turned out to be gallstones which had blocked the entrance to the gallbladder, causing massive infection, in fact very possibly a life-threatening condition and although I survived, it took many months to recover.

So my ministry came to an end, I lost my home, had to give up my children, and fought a life-threatening illness. The only thing that remained intact during those dark days was my job. The book of Job became my close companion and I learned a great deal through that amazing man.

It was during the time of convalescence that Jim very bravely came to visit me regularly and the headlong plunge into despair, decay and a future consisting of looking after someone else's cats in someone else's attic abruptly halted. Jim asked me to marry him and I moved out to 'Tununu' farm early in 1998 to a new beginning on a lovely farm with the greatest guy in the whole world.

It strikes me that there is more than mere coincidence in the fact that Jim's history has many similarities to my own. Both our families originated in Britain, and both moved out to Southern Africa to make a new life. Jim's father, Johnny (better known as Tommy) flew Lancaster Bombers in World War Two for the Royal Air Force and was eventually stationed in Rhodesia in 1943. After the war ended his superiors asked the men if any of them would like to stay and try their hand at tobacco farming.

Tommy decided to stay, and first worked as an assistant then as a manager on various farms around Salisbury, the capital city. He married Mavis who was a widow with three children, and a long-time friend. Together they moved out to the Tengwe block, which the government had opened up to new farmers. Tengwe was a completely deserted area at that time, so I am happy to say that in this particular area at least, nobody was thrown off their lands in order to make way for the white farmers.

Tengwe is a hot, dry and arid area, which does not enjoy huge rainfall. Also the soils there are schist soils and as such a very difficult to work. These two facts alone may account for Tengwe's lack of population, because it does need the technical expertise of dam construction and other water preservation methods, boreholes and the inclusion of additives to the soil in order to make farming, and therefore a living, possible.

Tommy and Mavis set up their farm called Tununu, and those were very hard days for the new farmers. Few were wealthy and life was simple. Hard but plenty of fun, too! The people who moved out there did so at roughly the same time. Everyone had a piece of virgin bush, with one free borehole per farm sunk by a benevolent government; but there were no roads, no electricity, no housing, and no comforts at all. Jim and his sister Linda were both born after the move to Tununu and became known as 'The Two *Nunu's.*'

Since there were no roads, each farmer initially 'signposted' the way to his farm using pieces of coloured cloths tied to trees. Every farmer used a different coloured cloth for easy reference to specific farms. Most started off by building and dwelling in pole and dagga huts for the first ten years or so, while they established 'compounds' for their African labourers, stumped and cleared lands, planted the first crops, built roads, built club and community church, and of course started their families.

Tommy and Mavis initially enjoyed a slightly more comfortable home, as they were able to afford a prefabricated one. Tommy often joked that although he started off well, somehow the other farmers all overtook him and in due course, built brick houses—while he was still living in a prefab one! Mavis' older son George was by then in his late teens. He chose a site for the house near the borehole, and constructed the house himself finally planting an orchard behind it.

'There is not much difference between a day in the life of a hippopotamus and a day in the life of a farmer's wife,' began Mike Mason, lounging comfortably on his bar stool, ice cold beer in hand, and smiling with his topaz coloured eyes. His hands, wrapped round the glass were strong, lean and bronzed by the sun; farmer's hands. The country club was filling up with its usual crowd of farmers decked on in khaki shorts and vellies (another form of bush shoe); the women wore gaily coloured sundresses, or high-cut shorts with strappy tops and floppy hats. Saturday was the day one could finish work early, come up to the club for a game of tennis, squash or touch rugby and finish up with dinner and a drink or two (or more depending on habitat and preferences!). Conversation would wash and swirl around the clubhouse along with the cigarette smoke, generally getting louder and rowdier as the evening wore on.

'And why is that?' I asked, somewhat taken aback by the analogy.

'Well, that's because they both sleep all day and eat all evening. The only difference actually is that the hippo has to forage for his own food, while the farmer's wife just sits and yells, "Cookie, boysa lo scoff!"' (Roughly translated means 'Cook please bring the dinner'). Nonplussed, I thought of Gran, Muz and Melan, all three farmers' wives of many years, who were always working very hard. If these farmer's wives didn't, then they were unlike any that I knew of, then again, if the hot blasts of air filtering in through the windows was anything to go by, I wasn't surprised. October time must be like wearing a fur coat—enough heat to drain even the zippiest energy. I probably looked a bit startled though, because Jim started to laugh. 'Don't pay too much attention to what Mike says,' he said.

Although Mike was the local comedian, he had a valid point. We did have a relatively good lifestyle including a barrage of house staff and gardeners who catered to our every wish, cooking, cleaning, gardening and the like. My whole day really was mine to fill with whatever activity took my fancy. Taking after the womenfolk of my family who have done it all before, my day was always fully occupied with something, but I was designing my life by doing exactly what I chose to do. Whilst it makes an excellent way of living, one could argue that it is not the best way of building character.

When Jim and I married early in 1998, I moved out to the small, relatively isolated farming district of Tengwe, complete with my luggage and my own expectations. Since my family had a farming background, to be a farmer's wife would be a great delight to me! My husband is a wonderful guy, but like most bachelors who are predominantly hunters and gatherers, his cottage needed a woman's touch. When your 'houseboy' tells you that you need new curtains because yours have holes in them, then you must know how large those holes have become.

There was plenty for me to do, and I looked forward to tackling my new home. I imagined myself in red-checked apron, admiring rows of jars of pickles and jams, fabric painting mornings spent with like-minded ladies, afternoon tennis and tea, shopping trips to the thriving metropolis of Westgate shopping center, Harare and the like. How we enjoyed those sorties to choose furnishings and fabrics, new curtains and pictures. We took measurements and designed our own bookshelves and room dividers. We built a cottage for my children and that also had to be decorated, and added several pets to our growing 'family'. Two guard dogs—a German shepherd and Great Dane, and two toy dogs—a Miniature Pinscher and a Jack Russell completed our home life. Talk about all creatures' great and small!

For the first time in my adult life, I was living in a home I could call my own, and that brought so much joy. There were some wonderfully fulfilling days setting up home together, redecorating Jim's cottage and designing, building and decorating the children's cottage. We had such pleasure visiting fabric and paint shops, matching carpeting and curtaining, combining both our household goods, decorating every available space, filling the verandah with pot plants. Jasmine, a longstanding favourite was planted along the verandah and the security fences. We dug new flowerbeds and planted new lawns. We absorbed piles of home and garden magazines for ideas. It was a slow-going and infinitely satisfying task.

Jim and I had a few hills to climb even in that tender first year of marriage, the hills of adjustment, change and loss. Adjustment and change because I came as a 'package deal' with three children entering into their teens—not an easy assignment for a man hitherto a bachelor. Like his father before him, he had to take a giant leap from being a household of one to a household of five, with all the attendant interests of young teenagers, and my three were certainly no exception. Loud music, sports kit tossed onto lounge chairs, nervous admirers and endless requests for permission to drive the farm pickup truck and go shooting with the .22 were standard. I think that they are the most wonderful kids in the whole world (no disrespect to all the other kids who go by the same title), but they are totally human, occasionally angelic, and sometimes a challenge.

One day Kimberley asked me, 'Why is it that parents and children get into so many arguments when children start learning to drive?'

'Why don't you get the keys of the pick-up truck and I'll just show you?' I answered. She figured out the reason before too long. When Robin started driving, I had to insist on a speed limit, even on the rutted, dusty farm roads!

Both Jim and I were used to doing things our own way, and for people in their late thirties to change sufficiently to accept someone else's way of doing things was sometimes difficult. Many days I gave the house and garden staff instructions whereupon Jim, returning from the fields, would simply issue another set of instructions. His staff, used to doing things his way, would change direction in favour of the 'Baas'.

African people were often hitch-hiking along the dirt roads of the deep farming communities where busses and taxis did not venture. Our sturdy pick-up trucks and 4 x 4's could cope with the rutted, potholed and dusty tracks. Not all farmers' wives were prepared to help out by giving them a lift, but I was quite happy to do so. Once they were riding in the back of my pick-up truck, they couldn't do me personally any harm. The only trouble was they were quite content to use the hubcaps as a hitch up onto the payload at the back and that is not what hubcaps are for.

'Where's the hubcap?' Jim asked me one day when I returned from a shopping sortie in our small Tengwe shopping centre which consisted of a few houses, a Farmer's Co-Op which smelt of sadza, dried kapenta, and Lifebouy soap, a butchery, a gift shop, a petrol station and a mechanic workshop. On the way home I'd stopped to give some labourers a lift.

'Oops,' I said stopping to frown and survey the space where the hubcap used to be. 'I've got no idea,' I added and then explained I'd given some Africans a lift.

'You'll have to go back and find it.'

That made me very grumpy, but I did as I was told. Of course I couldn't find it. You never can after something like that. But afterwards, whenever offering a lift to someone I'd always give an imperfect rendition of Shona and remind them, 'Basopa lo hubcaps!' and insist they get in at the back and not over the wheel wells.

One dry, hot day driving along one of the dusty farm roads, I saw a young African couple, loaded with bags and heading towards the main road. For me in the truck it was still at least 15 minutes away but for those two on foot, it was longer. I wasn't a cheerful giver, being hot, tired and longing to get home but I gave them a lift anyway issuing the standard, 'Basopa lo hubcaps' as I did so and watching them in the rear view mirror to ensure that they did so. They climbed in via the tailgate and we carried onto the main road.

When I got to the main road, I stopped to drop them off. The young woman came to the window and smiled. 'Datenda,' she thanked me and proffered a small bunch of bananas, a simple gesture that suddenly and without warning, broke my heart. You can't turn down such a gift. To do so would be unacceptably cruel practice. Giving them a lift had cost me nothing: I was going that way anyway. But giving me those bananas cost her plenty. So under the heat of the summer sun, the poor African woman blessed the rich white woman with a gesture I will never forget. But that was not all.

When I arrived home, Jim and Tim had returned from a shopping trip in Harare. They were unpacking the car and John, our Housekeeper was busy taking shopping bags into the house. Jim smiled at me and said, 'I got everything on your list, except for bananas. There weren't any in the supermarket. Can you believe it?'

'Well, wait until you hear what happened to me, and what I was given *buckshee* today!'

We ate those bananas with glad hearts knowing that they were a sacrifice of gratitude from someone we would probably never see again.

Jim's mum, Mavis was chronically ill with emphysema, and our wedding turned out to be her last outing. 'I don't feel very well,' she would say—remarkable statement considering she must have been feeling absolutely terrible. She couldn't breathe and constant dizziness bothered her a great deal. Her health deteriorated over the months, and we eventually said goodbye to her in the October of 1998.

'Sometimes I wished we had met before she became ill, because I never really got to know her as a person,' I told Jim one day.

'She had a gift for keeping family ties strong and for remaining calm in difficult moments,' he replied. 'She was good for my Dad.' He reminisced about her wonderful meals and fruity puddings. She was a dedicated mother and a loyal wife. I felt somehow I had missed something of value. So for both Jim and I, her passing was a great loss, but for different reasons.

It is often said that farmers put up security fences around their gardens not for the purpose of security, but to prevent their wives' gardens from encroaching into the lands! Our own security fence eventually enclosed about seven acres of ground, and yes we did extend it in order to build a cottage for the children, and to include some extra ground for gardening for myself.

'Don't ever plant anything outside the security fence. That's the absolute pits for any farmer's wife,' Mike my brother-in-law informed me one day. Maybe he was just rigid and inflexible.

'Why not?' I asked although the reason was obvious, I just wanted to hear him say it.

'Plenty of room inside it,' he replied, his gaze encompassing all seven-and-a-half acres inside it.

Naturally, I got Jim onsides and we did plant a number of trees, mostly jacarandas, outside the fence, ostensibly for shade over the cattle paddock as well as flowering trees for the beehives.

Moving into a new area means meeting many new people all at the same time, it's confusing and it takes time to sort them all out, find out who are the game-for-a-laugh ones, sporty ones, Christian ones; which women were friendly and which belonged to closed circles.

Jim had known all these people for many years, but I had to start from scratch. We became friendly with other farming folk in the area who also had teenage children, and who had the same interests as ours. They say that the accent may be on the youth, but the stress is still on the parents, and sharing ideas about teenage rearing with others in the same position was a great help. Our youngsters made several really good friends and together they explored the ups and downs in life. We formed a regular friendship with Lourens and Jan, our next-door neighbours. Lourens was all bushy gray hair and great gusts of belly-laughter. He funned and punned his way through social gatherings, dressing oddly enough to stand out. Jan, his pretty blonde wife had suffered some kind of bone disease as a youngster and had had to be put in traction for weeks. She still walked with a slight limp. Dirk and Shellynne, a good-looking couple with a similar background to ourselves, were bringing up Shellynne's three noisy boys also became good friends as did Brett and Lynne all of whom had teenage children. Brett was also a 'silent partner' in a viable and growing business in Harare, a venture that would eventually lead them away from the farm.

We also became great friends with Oscar and Leeann who were married the same year we were—through a common interest in setting up a new home, making new friends and pursuing new interests. Leeann became aerobics instructor at the club, and many were the hot afternoons she made us sweat it out in the club hall! 'Body and Soul' aerobics it was called.

1998 was also the year we established what we called our 'Compound Church'. There was much concern amongst the Christian communities that one of the most under-evangelized sectors of the population was the farms' 'compounds'. This was the collective term given to the groups of African people who lived and worked on the farms. A farmer from Karoi, Dave Richards was one of the original initiators of a drive to change this, sending out teams of evangelists into the farming districts to preach and teach at as many of the farms as would allow them. We were blessed to have the visiting team use our farm as a 'base' whilst they traveled around Tengwe. The Church they set up was truly blessed by the Lord, in that He continued to add regularly to their numbers those who were being saved—not only from our farm, but from neighboring farms and other settlements as well. It was a Church that was to feature so strongly during our time of trial as well.

Whilst 1998 was a year of adjustment, change and loss, 1999 was the only year of 'normal' times we were to enjoy. We visited some quiet pools of reflection that year, taking a short trip to the Eastern Highlands, Nyanga, Penhalonga and Chimanimani Mountains.

This trip came about thanks to the dentist, which may sound a little surprising!

'You need to have three wisdom teeth removed. In fact I'd really like to do it right now.'

I must have shrunk into that dentist's chair until I became invisible to the naked eye as a hundred stories of pain suffered after the removal of wisdom teeth sprang to instant recall. To make matters worse, x-rays revealed that the two lower wisdom teeth were impacted into the jawbone, necessitating removal of pieces of the said bone as well. There was no point hoping this was going to be relatively painless, but it did mean that anesthesia was necessary.

I do not recall too much about the day I went in for surgery, except watching Jim sitting in the early afternoon sunshine on the wide verandah outside the ward, drinking a cup of tea proffered by the nurse whilst I was under the 'Nil by Mouth' instructions. That cup of tea, despite the presence of sugar lurking in its depths, looked so incredibly tempting. My own intake was limited to a small plastic cup containing an assortment of tablets, to be taken with as little water as possible. Those tablets did their job so well; I was unconscious before the nursing staff even wheeled me into the operating theatre!

Later, the nurse came in bearing a Pethidine injection intended for killing pain. At least, this is my assumption because it is known as a 'pain killer'. However, that night, I found out why drug-induced 'highs' are also referred to as 'trips'. I must have ridden on every mode of transport ever devised by mankind—from horse-drawn carriage, to steam train, boat, aircraft—you name it, I rode on it. It was a very busy and active night, and I decided that Pethidine and I must come into contact less often. When the nurse came in the next morning carrying a small kidney-shaped bowl bearing another Pethidine-filled syringe, I politely turned it down.

'Ah, you are scared of injections,' she said, relishing the thought of a white woman's terror, African women are known to be much stronger physically.

'No, I just desperately need a rest.' She looked nonplussed. But my mouth was too sore to explain about the recent hectic trip were infinitely worse than the one I was about to take in the truck.

In order to take my mind off the pain, Jim took me away for a few days to the beautiful Eastern Highlands of Zimbabwe. Our first stop was the Chimanimani mountain range. The days were warm and sunny, the self-catering cottage, The 'Frog and Fern' was clean and comfortable, and happily situated to command a wonderful view of the mountains.

'More impressive than an All-Black lineout,' commented Jim admiring the mountain peaks that were standing tall and proud against the backdrop of the evening sky. Rugby was never far from his thoughts.

We visited the Vumba Mountains, returning to Eden Lodge where we had stayed for our honeymoon the previous year. Later we rounded off the trip in an old hotel, 'La Rochelle' in Penhalonga. The scenery was also beautiful but in a different way. The gardens were full of colourful trees, shrubs and flowers; some incredibly exotic and some local. We spent one afternoon at nearby nursery purchasing plants to take home as the beauty of the place had fired our imagination and enthusiasm over our own garden.

Amongst the plants we purchased were three tababuia trees and their presence played a significant part in the day we finally left Tununu for good. Tababuias have lovely leaves for most of the year, and for a very short time, usually in August as the weather is warming up for summer, they bud, and the flowers are an almost impossibly rich golden yellow. These flowers seem to last only about two weeks, but whilst they are there, they draw your attention like a magnet.

We planted our tababuias in a triangle shape to the right side of our verandah, and soon two of them, overjoyed to be in good solid ground shot up skyward in fine style. The other one, bemoaning its fate, simply remained where it was, stubbornly refusing to grow even one single inch taller. Perhaps it preferred the idea of being a bonsai special. Whatever the reason for its stunted growth I did not have the heart to take it out.

We also took the children on a 'round-Zimbabwe' trip that year, returning to Lake Kyle (now Mtilikwe) for the first time in twenty years—my old stamping-ground from the days of Rippling Waters. We took them to Great Zimbabwe ruins, where Kimberley got chased by a black mamba; several feet of aggression and sudden death before heading to Bulawayo and Matopos National Park. We stayed in a hunting camp with the delightful name 'Lebonka' where Maxin, the cook, treated us to an endless supply of delicious food. We ended up at Victoria Falls and in April, after a good rainy season, the Falls were every bit as spectacular as we had hoped. Looking back on it all, we were both thankful we had done that because a year later this kind of trip would not have been possible.

The Big Millennium caused great excitement around the world everywhere. We all wondered what the turn of the century would bring us, although most of us probably were not expecting any major change in our lives and simply enjoyed celebrating on a grand scale. And when our own were over, we watched those of others all over the world, courtesy of Television.

Little did we Zimbabweans realize that it would bring in its wake sudden, vicious and devastating change in the lives of millions around the country. For in destroying first the agricultural sector, followed by tourism and mining, as travelers became too terrified to visit, virtually every other Zimbabwean has suffered either directly or indirectly.

How was I to know that just two short years on our lives would change dramatically, or that our survival skills tested to the hilt and our marriage be placed under terrific strain? That by the time our fifth wedding anniversary came around, it would all be over, and we would celebrate in a land thousands of miles away? We never knew when it would be our turn to be harassed, or who would be harassed next, and what the outcome would be. Some people came out physically unharmed, others were beaten and tortured, and some were murdered. When it was your turn to be confronted, you did not know what to expect. Lastly, there was no set 'pattern' to the farm invasions, and nothing we could do to stop them, baffling because it all seemed such a pointless, needless waste.

Very shortly after the turn of the century, the country's President, Robert Mugabe, decided to hold a referendum. He wanted to be granted power to rule indefinitely, and the people were allowed to vote for or against the proposals put forward in that referendum.

The referendum was an unmitigated disaster for Mugabe. The turnout of voters was extremely poor—something that is normally considered indicative of a leader's unpopularity and of those who did cast their vote, the overwhelming majority voted against the proposals. He could not believe that these people whom he had fought so hard to set free were no longer backing him. 'The whites have turned my people have turned against me,' he said. How could they do this of their own free will? And he began to look around for a suitable 'escape route'. Whichever way we face what happened, he was way ahead of us in the plan he put together.

A scapegoat is always essential when something goes wrong, because you must never take the blame yourself. A minority group is a good scapegoat. That is nothing new in history—it has been done before. The land issue, which had not been properly addressed for twenty years, could become the pivotal issue. The government had long since lost interest in acquiring arable farmland, despite Britain's offer to help with the payment. Since 1980 if you wanted to sell your farm, you had to offer it to the government first. They would either buy it, whereupon it would be immediately abandoned, or they would give you a 'Certificate of No Interest' without which you could not sell your farm to someone else.

Nevertheless, the white farmers could become the scapegoats, and punishment would be inflicted on those who voted against him that day. The fact that the economy would be destroyed was of no real consequence apparently . . .

Shortly after the referendum the farm invasions began and life turned upside down. Devastating loss and tragedy followed. The first signs of trouble came from a farming district called Norton, but hard on the heels of those, many other areas were invaded as well as the movement gathered momentum. More and more youngsters, who had nothing to do with the Liberation Struggle, joined the 'war veterans' and with incredible speed the hostility and mayhem increased. Then came the day our worst fears were realized when we were told that a farmer had been murdered.

It was a Sunday morning, and we were gathering outside the Tengwe Community Church warming up in the early morning sunshine, waiting for the Anglican minister, Rob Haarhoff, to arrive from Chinhoyi to take the monthly Anglican service. He rolled up in his white pickup truck, blowing up a cloud of red dust even though he was going slowly. He got out and collected all his paraphernalia as we greeted him. Then he turned and looked at us. I knew that look from years before, on Bob Hill's face when Fred had died and my stomach twisted into a painful knot.

And it was Rob who broke the devastating news to us. I was grateful that at least if such terrible tidings had to be delivered, that it was delivered by a compassionate man of God, who cared deeply for his flock. Rob's congregations consisted largely of farmers, and he felt our suffering with us.

'A farmer was murdered last night. I don't have any other details. I don't know who he was or where it happened. But the death of anybody in such circumstances is a terrible tragedy. You will all need to be strong for what still lies ahead.'

I sat in the pew between Jim on one side and Laurie Dawson on the other, lost in my own world, sensing and seeing them but unable to connect; wanting only to stay there and weep for a long, long time, while the dust of the ages slowly seeped downwards, settling over everything that is precious in life and covering it with a layer of dull, monochrome futility and hopelessness. Then I wanted to go home and sleep for many hours. It was one of those moments in life where one is so totally helpless, so drained. He might not be anyone we knew, but his loss would be felt all the same, because he was one of us. There was no comfort anywhere; not in the fresh white-washed walls of the little country church, the words of the minister standing behind the pulpit praying for the right words to say, the subdued singing of the hymns, the sunshine spilling in through the windows. Where would we find God in all this?

It was brought home so sickeningly to us that morning, not only had someone lost his life, but also that this thing that was happening to us farmers, was terribly, terribly serious. We were plunged neck-deep in the chilly floodwaters with no way of being rescued. That was the first breath; the first realization of how this was going to end had hit us . . .

I kept our palm leaf crosses from that Palm Sunday service and stuck them on the study wall, where they stayed until we finally left Tengwe. They reminded us of the sacrifice that Jesus had made for us, but that year they also reminded us of other deaths.

We watched the BBC news and learned details of the torture and death of Dave Stevens the first farmer to lose his life, as well as the other farmers who died, and every time we saw them we prayed for those families whose losses were so very severe. We saw Maria Stevens, newly widowed in a deep pink jersey, her glossy auburn hair a striking contrast and those four young children gathered around her, so suddenly fatherless and so badly traumatized by the sudden turn of events.

'What do you remember most about your husband at this moment?' The BBC news reporter asked her gently.

'He was a *moral* man,' she spoke the word slowly and clearly, the inference and the contrast between him and the perpetrators of the crime was so obviously drawn.

Every day we tuned into the BBC news broadcasts to see what else was happening. It would be many years before I could hear the BBC's signature tune before the news without remembering the death of Dave Stevens and feeling the dread of what else it might bring.

That lunchtime, I opened a bottle of wine. The fragrance of other, sweeter, happier summers rose up from its mouth. These grapes were grown; this wine had been made and matured and even purchased well before any of the horror had begun.

Many Zimbabweans began to pray regularly and fervently that God would be merciful in their time of plight. The whole situation became so serious, so enveloping and with such speed, that we could only believe that if deliverance was going to come at all, it was going to come from On High. Surely nobody but God could deliver us from this terror.

Our next-door neighbour, Trevor Tiltman, slow talking, gentle-natured, almost self-sufficient farmer and a virtual hermit, landed right in the proverbial cactus, when his farm was designated for fast-track resettlement. Literally overnight, many settlers moved onto his farm and settled all over it, on the lands, in the bush, by the dam, and near the house. They began cutting down the trees for housing, ripping up the fences, destroying crops, and causing endless and unnecessary trouble for Trevor. It meant that Trevor was unable to plant a crop that coming season.

At that stage few of the farms in our immediate area had been so adversely affected, and as we were still able to carry on, we formulated a plan to help Trevor. Together with Lourens and Jan next door, we each offered Trevor some of our fallow lands so that he could plant a crop and carry on farming. It meant he had to spend quite a bit of time traveling around in his yellow land rover backwards and forwards between the two farms and split up his labour force, but he managed to cope very well, circumstances considered.

This was one of the best treasures, which came out of the continual trauma of the situation, the incredible unity we had with one another. Each farmer did his best by his neighbour, and we bonded together in a way that people can only do when their livelihoods and even their very lives are threatened. I believe that this is one of the biggest reasons why, right at the end, the parting of ways was so incredibly painful. Parting is painful anyway, but it was made more so by this bonding the hard times caused.

We still had the same 'Agric-Alert' type radios on the farms; both wall units in the houses and hand-held ones the farmers carried about with them, and at regular intervals it would crackle into life as one of the farmers would inform us, 'We have a situation developing on . . . farm, please could everyone come and provide some support.' Whereupon as many farmers as possible would drop what they were doing, get into their pickup trucks and drive to the farm concerned to just simply give an added presence as groups of 'war vets' or 'wovvits' as we called them gathered on farms to 'shupa' the farmer. Crowds of angry Africans, sometimes drunk or drugged, breaking things down, burning things, using farmers' pets for target practice, angry rhetoric, spears, poles, sometimes guns and a lot of 'toy-toying' (a dance Africans do when they are angry). One particularly stroppy 'war vet' who called himself 'Rex Jesus' stole a hand-held radio from someone and used it to great effect usually in the middle of the night, threatening to murder all the white farmers in the area.

We could do absolutely nothing to protect ourselves and this presence was simply a show of solidarity. Farming became increasingly difficult and for the men whose God-give role it is to protect and provide for their families, having these mandates taken away from them was devastating to their self esteem. For women who are bearers of life, nurturers, and home-makers it was also difficult because our children could no longer roam around the farms and how could we make nice homes when we had no idea how long we'd be able to stay in them? Some people were given just an hour or half and hour to pack up and go, some were forced off with threats of hostility and violence. And some were murdered.

Initially, foreign journalists were allowed on the farms to interview both farmers and wovvits. One perplexed British journalist got to interview Mrs Rusike, Head of the 'War Veterans Widows Association' and she told him; 'The white people came up from South Africa in 1891 in their Land Rovers. When they ran out of fuel, they just parked the Land Rover and claimed all the land around it.' She described wide sweeps of land with her hands.

'What am I supposed to do if I lose my land?' the farmer asked, frustrated and angry. Rhetorical question really, as no-one had any ready answers, but most especially not someone who thought there were Land Rovers in 1891.

One day Agritex, a firm in Karoi, sent people to peg out some of the farms for resettlement purposes, ours included. It was a day we had hoped would not happen, and we confined ourselves to the homesteads whilst they went about their business.

The farm was duly pegged into twenty plots, and each plot was given a number. That number was painted onto any handy object like a fence post, rock or tree. Then the corresponding numbers were written onto forms and handed out to twenty settlers who had applied for land. The men left, satisfied with the task they had performed, and we waited for the outcome.

The first settler did not take long to make his appearance. He arrived in a seriously clapped-out vehicle filled with his wife, two children and pitifully sparse possessions. They drove that vehicle deep into the shaded woods around the dam and built themselves a hut of thatching grass, and anything else that the land could provide. And they were determined to make our lives as uncomfortable as possible without actually resorting to violence. That was another regularly employed tactic on many farms—many things they did were not violent, but sometimes the aim was pure and simple annoyance value. Building their huts on your driveway so you had to drive around them, setting things on fire, uprooting crops as they were being planted or singing outside your security fence all night so that you cannot sleep, will not hurt you, but it will cause serious annoyance and is designed to bring out the worst in you.

The man did not remain for long, but left his wife to her own devices whilst he went back to Karoi. We had only one run-in with them, which had the potential to become violent; the rest of the run-ins were simply irritating.

Although she was most likely a simply schooled peasant woman, this lady cottoned on very quickly to the fact that the farmer could be considered as a goose to lay golden eggs. She only had to figure out a way of commandeering as many of these golden eggs herself. She did not have her husband around, so she turned to the local 'war veteran' leader, Machaka, for help. Together they concocted ways of extracting money from us.

Machaka arrived one morning with the said lady and said, 'Your cattle broke into this woman's house while she was out and they ate all her maize meal. What are you going to do about it?' Machaka's hair was a filthy dust-bath of knotty old dreadlocks, his breath smelled like an ancient tomb and his eyes were bloodshot but still able to glare through you like a knife-blade—much like the terrorists of the bush war. His clothes were equally filthy.

We were highly skeptical of this since cattle do not normally enter into dwellings to take food supplies, especially when a plentiful food supply is close to hand.

'How much maize did she have? I will replace it with some of our maize meal,' Jim replied calmly, trading the man stare for stare. He couldn't believe the amount of maize she apparently had. 'It would take her years to eat that much maize,' he said to me afterwards.

'She doesn't want your maize. She wants money instead.' *No arguments, no compromise; just hand over buddy and make it snappy before I call my gang of thugs.*

Jim did pay her compensation, although the sum she insisted on was simply wicked. He decided however, not to run the risk of having the same complaint again, and took tractor, materials and labourers, and they erected a fence around her plot.

'Why she has to have her hut inside the cattle paddock, heaven only knows. There are plenty of other places she could have built it.'

'Maybe she just liked the view,' I snorted and stomped off to find something more worthwhile to do.

Later on, she dug a piece of ground and planted vegetable seeds in it. For some reason she did this outside the fence, with the result that she once again had problems with the cattle, which unsurprisingly, stood on the seedlings and squashed them. Once again she arrived with Machaka the Ultimate Black Mamba, complete with forked tongue and filled with deadly venom, demanding an audience with Jim.

'Your cattle have crushed all her vegetables.'

'Tell her she's welcome to come every day and get some fresh vegetables from the garden,' Jim offered, waving a hand in the general direction of the vegetable garden and Babbiton's curly head just visible above the showy greenery.

"She doesn't want your vegetables,' Machaka's voice rose several decibels. 'She wants money!'

'Why am I surprised?'

She once again, insisted on a huge sum of money as compensation. 'What do you do? It is like trying to deal with a hijacker who is holding a gun to your head. He is unreasonable, and uninterested in your point of view,' Jim came in, and taking off his floppy hat, wiped his forehead with a grease-stained handkerchief. 'It's pointless keeping the cattle. She's just going to keep on using them as an excuse for compensation. Besides, other plot owners will start pitching up. There'll be no grazing for them.'

So, shortly afterwards the cattle were sold for slaughter. This was particularly heartbreaking because most of the cows were in calf. Our bulls affectionately named Jethro, Damocles, Sparticus and Barak went with them. So the lady in question could no longer use the misdeeds of our cattle as a way of extracting money out of us. Later on, we also left. She has her piece of land, but the easy source of income is gone. I sometimes wonder if she is still there and how she is coping.

Machaka was joined by another 'war vet' leader, Sicha. Whereas Machaka was like a black mamba, with cold gleaming eyes, vile aggression and ready to strike at any moment, Sicha was clean, neatly dressed, polite, well-spoken and almost a gentleman except he still wanted all the farms in the area. They had a group of rough hangers-on who had nothing better to do than roam from farm to farm harassing farmers, pulling up crops, killing cattle and shuparing the farm labourers.

We finally left the farm on a dry, windy day in August 2002, never to return. Sicha, Machaka and their grubby hangers-on watched the proceedings from dawn onward, making sure we paid all the labourers their massive 'severance pay' packages that the government demanded, and finally making sure we got off the farm altogether. Jim gave Sicha and Machaka a Gideon bible each, telling them that we did not hold what they had done against them. The labour force, unwanted and uncared for, certainly by the *wovvits* would be leaving soon after. The jasmine creepers were choc-full of fat pink buds. Another day or so and they would open into delicately tinted white flowers and fill the air with their perfume. The pair of golden orioles, an inter-Africa migratory species had returned for the summer and were filling the air with their joyous, liquid-gold calls.

Dad, Muz, and Melan came to help, packing up furniture and clothes and distributing cups of tea and sandwiches. Never since John's death had the family been gathered together in such solemn silence.

At one point Jim came to me and said, 'I want to show you something.' He took me by the hand into the garden to where the tababuias were covered in their rich golden-yellow flowers and pointing downwards to the stubborn little bonsai-special, I saw that it too, for the first time was sporting three beautiful golden flowers. Tears pricked my eyes. It had survived harsh conditions to flower beautifully; three flowers reminded me of God the Father, God the Son and God the Holy Spirit who, in this touching scene, gave me hope and courage that we too, brutally uprooted as we were, would transplant elsewhere in the world to bloom beautifully once again.

The debate, about who the land belongs to, continued to rage. Everyone had some opinion they could express, and the big question of prime farmland taken from the African people years ago still remained. It is a wrong that should be made right—only making it right with another wrong is not, nor ever was, the solution.

If one wanted to go back further in history, then the rightful 'owners' of the land were once the San Bushmen who now live in the Kalahari Desert further south. The Shona people chased the Bushmen of their land and claimed it as their own!

I will only cite one example of how this debate raged, because this one made a particular impact upon us at the time. One of the farmer's wives from Karoi, Joy Straarup was working in the African store on their farm when a 'war veteran' came in to buy some goods. When he saw the white farmer's wife was in the store, he must have decided that this was a good opportunity for a confrontation.

He started getting into a discussion with her about stealing land from the rightful owners, and to prove his point, pulled an old, worn Gideon Bible out of his pocket. Turning to 1 Kings 21: 1-16, he read the story of Naboth, Queen Jezebel and King Ahab out loud to Joy—and God's viewpoint about people who steal land from other people.

'You see, Queen Jezebel and King Ahab stole Naboth's land, *and look what happened to them!'* he told her.

Quickly, Joy turned the tables on him, using the same story to prove her point and said, 'Yes, they took Naboth's land *and look what happened to them!'*

I confess to being impressed that this 'war veteran' knew the story of Naboth, because it is quite an obscure story. You rarely hear it quoted, or spoken about. It seemed to me to be an indicator that this man must have known his Bible rather well. Yet opposite sides could use the same story to prove diametrically opposing points! Which raises the crucial question: Whose land is it anyway?

The frightening reality about the concept of 'truth' is that it can become a relative term in the hands of different people who have opposing viewpoints. In John 14: 6 Jesus said, 'I am the way, *the truth*, and the life. No one comes to the Father but through Me'. Jesus Himself is the absolute, ultimate and living truth. We can only know what The Truth really is if we are linked to its Source—Jesus. If we are alive in Christ and He is living in us, then we can discern what truth is. For truth is not merely a concept, it is a person and without that person, Jesus, in our lives the truth can at best be only a relative thing, and at worst it can become seriously distorted.

Scripture tells us that 'the earth is the Lord's and all its fullness, the world and all those who dwell therein. For He has founded it upon the seas, and established it upon the waters' (see Psalm 24: 1, 2).

In the gospel of Matthew from chapter 13 onwards, Jesus told a number of 'kingdom parables', each one explaining a different aspect of the kingdom of God, and they very clearly illustrate this truth. This land is not ultimately ours. Even if we did pay for it. Even if there was nobody living there before. This land belongs to God and we are simply stewards of His great wealth. He has entrusted His belongings to us, to do what we will, until His return.

Owning a piece of land—legally or otherwise—does not mean we can do with that land what we please. We used our farm in Zimbabwe to grow crops and raise cattle. The commodities we produced provided much-needed foreign revenue for the country and food to feed the nation (as well as other nations around). It also provided homes, jobs and fields for the sixty families who lived there and worked for us.

We never took our African labourers for granted, because they were important to us. Without them we could not have run the farm as we did—we would have been helpless, stuck. Each family on the farm had at least one person working for us although many of the wives were also employed. They all had brick houses and they were given a home and a piece of land of their own to work. We provided them with seed and fertilizer for their own crops. The top-paid labourers had electricity in their houses.

We had a crèche for the children, and a health worker to look after the more minor ailments, and to make sure there was ongoing education on topics such as AIDS. We built up a Church, and organized a soccer team. We provided the soccer team with sports kit, a field and tractors and trailers for transport for 'away' matches on other farms. We used to regularly send labourers to attend courses at the local agricultural college to improve and increase their knowledge and skills. In short we did what we could to improve their lot in life. This was not unusual, and many farmers did even more than all this.

Where are those labourers now? What has become of them? No matter how heavy the losses we have sustained have been, theirs have been infinitely worse. I say this in the sense that we will find a new place to live, a new job, and a new school for the children. We will still have a roof over our heads, and food to eat. Hard as it may be to make the adjustment, life will go on.

Most people recognized the need for land reform. Many farmers were willing to assist with the process. In our area alone there were six abandoned farms, all of which could have been restored to useful capacity with financial and technical assistance, as well as the working knowledge of those who'd farmed for years. We could have made it a 'team effort' to support new farmers make a go of it without their going bust in the first season. Our own labour forces, who knew a good deal about farming, would have made a great place to start. None of us would ever have pushed them into the future they were given, which was in effect, much like signing their death warrants.

These labourers face a bleak future, or possibly some of them will have no future at all. They will swell the ranks of the 'landless peasants' and will have no jobs, no homes and no food. Their immune systems will be weakened by lack of food and proper care, and many who would have otherwise survived, will die. The average life expectancy of a man had dropped to 37 years and for a woman, just 34 years. That means an increasing number of AIDS orphans being taken care of by aged grandparents. Finally the horrors of 2000 and the Government's 'Fast track land resettlement Programme' which put paid to the farming sector virtually overnight, also short-circuited the tourism and thereafter by anything worthwhile. Zimbabwe went from the 'Breadbasket of Africa' to a 'Basket Case' could boast of nothing more than the world's fastest-shrinking economy and is now rated one of the worst places to live, outstripping even Afghanistan. The life expectancy of the average man is 37 years, and the average woman, just 34.

'The earth is the Lord's and all its fullness. The world and all those who dwell therein.' Whoever 'owns' the land has a responsibility towards God, and towards His people to do what is right by Him, by them and by it.

POTHOLES 'BELOW THE SURFACE'

THE VALLEY OF ACHOR, A DOOR OF HOPE

From Hosea Chapter Two

'Rebuke your mother, rebuke her,
For she is not my wife,
And I am not her husband.
Let her remove that adulterous look from her face
And the unfaithfulness from between her breasts.
Otherwise I will strip her naked
And make her as bare as on the day she was born;
I will make her like a desert,
Turn her into a parched land,
And slay her with thirst.
I will not show my love to her children,
Because they are children of adultery.
Their mother has been unfaithful
And has conceived them in disgrace.
She said, "I will go after my lovers;
Who give me my food and water,
My wool and my linen, my oil and my drink."
Therefore I will block her path with thorn bushes;
I will call her so that she cannot find her way.
She will chase after her lovers but not catch them;
She will look for them but not find them.

Then she will say,
I will go back to my husband as at first,
For then I was better off than now.'
She has not acknowledged that I was the one
Who gave her the grain,
The new wine and oil,
Who lavished on her the silver and gold—
Which they used for Baal.

Therefore I will take away my grain when it ripens
And my new wine when it is ready.
I will take back my wool and my linen,
Intended to cover her nakedness.
So now I will expose her lewdness before the eyes of her lovers;
No one will take her out of my hands.
I will stop all her celebrations:
Her yearly festivals, her new Moons,
Her Sabbath days—all her appointed feasts.
I will ruin her vines and her fig trees,
Which she said was her pay for her lovers:
I will make them a thicket and wild animals will devour them.
I will punish her for the days
She burned incense to the Baals;
She decked herself with rings and jewellery
And went after her lovers, but Me she forgot,'
Declares the Lord.

*'***Therefore I am going to allure her;***
I will lead her into the desert and speak tenderly to her.
There I will give her back her vineyards,
And will make the Valley of Achor a door of hope.
There she will sing as in the days of her youth,
As in the days she came up out of Egypt.

In that day,' declares the Lord,
'You will call Me, "My husband";
You will no longer call Me, 'My Master.'

This amazing declaration by God comes from a broken heart, from which unbroken love is still springing forth. When love is too deep for mere words, then we use poetry and song, and our wonderful God does the same so many times when He is declaring His undying love for us.

To understand where this comes from, though, we do need to know where the Valley of Achor is and its significance to Israel. Way back Joshua chapter 7 we find that Achor is synonymous with moral failure. Israel were preparing to enter the Promised Land and had launched their first massive campaign against Jericho, a campaign that was a resounding success, despite the long process and strange instructions, God won a decisive victory.

Before the battle however, God had given Israel a set of very specific instructions. The spoils of the city were sacred and belonged to God and the people were not to touch any of it. But Achan, one man, just one individual out of an entire nation found the temptation to do so just too strong for him and he helped himself to some silver, gold and a robe, all of which he buried under the floor of his tent.

Nobody knew about it and God Himself said nothing until the next battle which was against a very small city called Ai. The Israelites should have won the battle hands down, but they lost. And Joshua knew then that there was something wrong between God and His chosen people. Joshua put on sackcloth and ashes and pleaded with Almighty God to reveal to him what the problem was, and God revealed Achan's sin. Joshua got all the leaders together and they took Achan and his entire family and executed them in a valley, and buried them there. Sad to say, but sin can and does, have a knock-on effect on the people around us. In this case, the sin of one man affected a whole nation, and a whole family perished as a result.

'Achor' actually means 'trouble' or 'violating a ban' and for Israel, the Valley of Achor became a place of dark shame in the nation's history.

As I studied these verses from Hosea, they took my mind back to a time and place many years previously in Israel's history, when the Lord had delivered her from the bondage of slavery in Egypt and Miriam led the Israelites in a massive praise and worship service. What a service that must have been!

Through all the years that followed; years spattered with Israel's grumbling, wandering, rebellion, faithlessness and resultant exiles and embrace of foreign gods, there was never a time when God forgot that night of praise and worship.

At the time when Hosea was written, the worship of Yahweh, the one true God and that of Baal had become so mixed up and so confusing, people did not always realize who they were actually worshipping. Through all the sludge, the Lord remembered the sweetness of their praise and worship. Although Israel had broken His heart, His love remained constant and unchanged; unbroken. Just as the song remained a constant, unchanged memory for Him whose heart yearned to take her to a place of restoration, and she would sing to Him as she had in the days of her youth.

It may seem like such a paradox that instead of leading her away from the place of shame, He leads her straight back to it. I wonder why the Lord would do something like that? Insofar as we can understand a holy God, and why He would choose to do such a thing, perhaps we will not know or understand the amazing depths of His love unless we know what it is He has delivered us from.

Valleys are places where the fertilizer is, where we learn things, not only about the world around us, but also about ourselves. And no matter what darkness, hopeless situation people find themselves in, there is always a Door of Hope that leads out from the valley; there is an escape. Jesus Christ is the door through which we pass to escape, and once we do, we will sing massive songs of praise and worship once again, because no matter what we do or how bad we are, God has, in love provided a way out.

God uses this valley for Israel the nation to gently restore what she has lost and He does the same for us as individuals, whether Jew or Gentile. It is the last place that anyone would expect to find a door of hope.

And yet, if you look at the three 'therefores', which I have highlighted, you will see that the first two positively reverberate with judgement, and when the last one comes, you expect one final blast of judgement and instead, you get completely blown away by the tranquillity of the picture that the words paint: *"Therefore I am now going to allure her, I will lead her to the desert and speak tenderly to her. There I will give her back her vineyards, and will make the Valley of Achor a door of hope."*

I read this and once and for all, it tells me that God's mercy triumphs over judgement and this is positive proof that although the Lord may get angry, His anger burns out and all that is left is mercy. The Lord does not want to judge us in anger, because then all we will turn into is shivering, gibbering wrecks worthy of nothing but eternal damnation, which He would have to do if we were under the Law. He wants to hear us sing songs of praise and enjoy His presence, and that is why He deals with us in grace, and why mercy triumphs over judgement.

In all, there are three women involved in this moving saga of people's foolishness, God's judgement, mercy and grace. The first is Miriam. No matter was transpired in the desert for her, after that night of the thundering triumph of praise, this was the event for which she is remembered and the one that left its mark on the very heart of God.

Then there was Hosea's wife. Hosea was himself commanded by God to take a harlot for a wife. In those days the penalty for adultery was severe—adulteresses were taken outside the city gates and stoned to death. Yet God commanded Hosea to take Gomer, the adulterous wife, back into his home. No doubt many of the men of his time must have thought Hosea had gone soft in the head, and he must have been the butt of some cruel jokes and vicious sport. Hosea's life with his harlot wife was meant to be a parallel of what God had been suffering through the harlotry of Israel.

God even chose names for his children that were meant to exemplify that He no longer blessed them. The first, a son, was named 'Jezreel' because God was soon to punish the house of Jehu for the massacre at Jezreel. The second, a daughter, was called 'Lo-Ruhamah' signifying that God would no longer show love for Israel (although He still showed love to Judah). Gomer produced another son called 'Lo-Ammi' meaning they were not His people and He was not their God. When Gomer was restored to Hosea, then God changed these names. This can sound like a very dry-as-dust account, but I am sure that Gomer must have experienced a maelstrom of emotions, including the deepest, darkest shame that can only be found in the Valley of Achor.

Nakedness in a physical sense can be a humiliating thing. When Adam and Eve fell, the first thing that happened was that they lost their innocence, and realizing they were naked, made fig leaves (signifying the works of their own hands) to cover themselves. Fear and shame came into being as new players in the human dilemma. But it was more a picture of spiritual nakedness. Spiritual nakedness can be even more humiliating, because from fig leaves upwards, there is absolutely nothing to hide behind. God slew the first innocent animal (a picture of grace) to make covers for them. And here, years later, Gomer must have felt this so keenly, with a husband who was a prophet and therefore had a high standing in the community and was reasonably well-known, plus children who also had a share in her shame.

The last woman mentioned, is of course, God's chosen nation, Israel and we remember that she is a parallel of His church. Although I have used these verses to share what we go through in a personal sense, there is also another sense in which they are true and that is the parallel with Israel, the nation. Someday Israel will also enjoy restoration with God. Today the Valley of Achor is a desert, a place of fighting, skirmishing and all the attendant horrors of war. I look forward to the day when that, too, is restored to all that God once had in mind and we can gaze on beauty that has been given in place of ashes. All of us, as His Church or as His chosen nation, will once again in response to His love lift our voices in a mighty praise and worship service.

What is your Valley of Achor today? Commit it to the Lord and trust in all that He has waiting for you as He takes it away and replaces the ashes of your life for the beauty in His.

POTHOLES 'SHORT THOUGHTS'

'. . . AND IT CAME TO PASS . . .'

The man standing on the podium ready to give the first talk of the day looked so lost, so alone, and he'd just made himself very vulnerable by describing the demise of his farm, and his family. How he'd managed to get through that and still be upright even was a miracle. He spoke with such an amazingly strong voice, but it was gut wrenching all the same.

His family owned probably the hugest farm we passed on our way from Tengwe to Harare, and to see those large wheat fields every year was always a joy. So many people had been provided with bread from those fields, but that was over as the 'war vets' had moved in on the prime fields and taken over.

We all lived on our farms, so when we lost them we lost our homes also—everything gone and nothing given back in return. But this man, I'll call him Allan, had had to contend with another heartbreak since it happened. His wife, Debbie, had woken up early one Sunday morning and realized to her extreme concern that she could not move her legs.

Allan bundled her into the car and rushed her to the family Doctor, but he had no idea what the problem could be and referred them to a Neurologist. The diagnosis came back—Polyneurosis. Polyneurosis or 'guillian-barre syndrome' as it is also known is a rare but deadly disease caused by a malfunction of the autoimmune system. It usually starts with either tingling or paralysis in the legs which quickly spreads up to the arms and upper body. As long as only involuntary muscles are affected, the victim will survive, but when the involuntary muscles (such as those that control the diaphragm) are affected, then it becomes life-threatening.

For Debbie, the disease advanced unabated, and despite the best possible care, the paralysis spread slowly upward until the only movement she had was opening and closing her eyelids. Six weeks later, she died.

'I'm not a Christian in the accepted sense,' he concluded, 'but I find great comfort in the scripture verse, "and it came to pass".' Can you imagine how much worse this would all be if it was here to stay?'

If the nightmare situations in which we find ourselves would never change, life probably wouldn't be worth living. I know that as Christians we might be tempted to say he'd used the scripture verse out of context; charmingly, courageously, perhaps, but also incorrectly. Yet it still reflects a great scriptural truth. Seasons do come . . . and eventually pass also. They change! Ecclesiastes chapter 3 deals with this very thing. There is a time for every purpose under heaven:—

> *To everything there is a season,*
> *A time for every matter under heaven:*
> *A time to be born, and a time to die;*
> *A time to plant, and a time to pluck up what is planted.*

A time to kill, and a time to heal;
A time to break, down and a time to build up;
A time to weep, and a time to laugh;
A time to mourn, and a time to dance;
A time to throw away stones, and a time to gather stones together;
A time to embrace, and a time to refrain from embracing;
A time to seek, and a time to lose;
A time to keep, and a time to throw away;
A time to tear, and a time to sew;
A time to keep silence, and a time to speak;
A time to love, and a time to hate;
A time of war, and a time of peace.

Finally in the day of evil, you can also claim the powerful promise from Isaiah 59: 19 as the memory verse:—

'When the enemy comes in like a flood, the Spirit of the Lord will raise up a standard against him.'

The Holy Spirit is the Standard Bearer. The standard He raises is the Lord Jesus Christ.
We gather together underneath that Standard.

GOD WILL ALWAYS HAVE THE FINAL SAY
HE'S HAD IT SINCE BEFORE THE FOUNDATION
OF THE WORLD

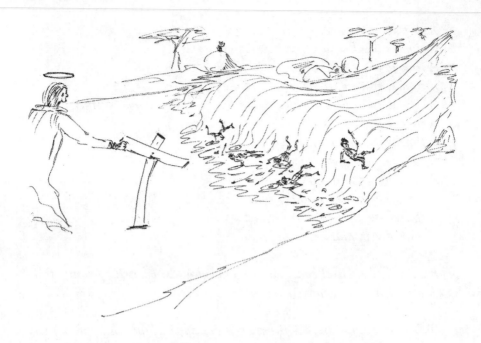

POTHOLES 'SHORT THOUGHTS'

'YOU PREPARE A TABLE BEFORE ME IN THE PRESENCE OF MY ENEMIES'

Psalm 23: 5

Lance and Janet roll their eyes dramatically at each other across the intervening space of Michael and Rhoda's garden. 'Do lally' definitely 'do lally' is mirrored on each set of features and they might be right.

Michael and Rhoda are dressed up Michelin Man-style against the snowy cold, their beanies almost covering their eyes. But they are singing cheerfully as they begin dusting the layer of powdery snow off various items in the garden. The bright red covers of the garden furniture reappear under Rhoda's vigorous brushing. Michael was busy cleaning up the big, black Weber and then inexplicably began filling it with kindling and wood. Rhoda set the table with cutlery, glasses and brought out a salad and foil-covered baked potatoes. Michael fired up the barbeque and they chatted amiably whilst they waited for the flames to die down enough to cook the meat.

'What are you going to use as ice for your drinks?' chuckled Janet, unable to resist a jibe. 'There are plenty of icicles hanging from your rooftop.'

'Want to come and join us?' Janet asked, 'there's plenty plus to eat here.'

'No thanks,' Janet said and giving Lance one last dramatic eye-roll she disappeared indoors, defeated by the intense cold. Lance couldn't resist watching to see what would actually happen so he lingered. He wanted to be sure to give an honest report about these weird neighbours of his, cheering himself with thoughts of hilarity. Michael and Rhoda were Christians and always finding alternative ways of doing things that nobody really understood, but this outdoor Barbie-in-the-snow was their finest example to date.

The barbie got underway and clouds of fragrant smoke rose heavenward. Soon Michael and Rhoda were ready to sit down to their meal. Lance turned to go indoors when something cold splashed onto the back of his neck and he realized to his consternation that the snow was indeed beginning to thaw.

Up above another sun broke through the wintry cold, its rays of coruscating warmth radiating down onto the garden below, transforming the scene from a hushed white world into the bosky green lushness of a spring day. The crescendo of birdsong grew vying with the cheerful laughter in the garden below as it filled with flowers of yellow, blue and red. And it was all contained in one yard; that of Michael and Rhoda. Their merriment continued unabated throughout their meal and long after they'd gone indoors, the fragrance of their festivities continued to hang on the still air.

Lance watched and waited but instead of mirth, something deep stirred inside it. What was it? A longing, a yearning to know what motivated these two strange people? Who was this God of theirs who could not be explained? Janet saw it and hated every moment of it. There was no logic or reason for her hatred, except the happiness of two people whose lives simply exposed her own misery.

High above, the angels sheathed their swords and watched this human activity, searching, probing into the invisible substrata, seeing and understanding far more than any human. They had just enjoyed a good rout against God's enemies and the skies were once again clear.

Their charges, Michael and Rhoda had strong faith in God, despite the persecution, the ugly rumours and unnecessary hardships imposed on them by those who did not understand. They stood upon promises like, *'You prepare a table before me, in the presence of my enemies'* and they knew and loved God well enough to know that He would indeed live up to His promises. Setting up a lunch table in the snow just proved His love, His response to their faith, both in season and out of season.

POTHOLES 'JOY BAG'

BEING AND DOING

'*To be is to do*'—Socrates

'*To do is to be*'—Satre

'*To be or not to be , that is the question,*'—'Hamlet' (Shakespeare)

'*Do Be Do Be Do Be*'—Frank Sinatra

You are a human BEING not a human DOING. Salvation is about BEING saved; it's not about DOING saved. Christianity is not about doing work, it's about a work that has been done. All you have to DO is BE-lieve! Only believe!

MOTHER'S DAY DEDICATION

A letter I received from my daughter some years ago contained a collection of sayings guaranteed to make me giggle.

Dearest Muz,

I found this sheet the other day, with some discoveries about growing older. I'll reproduce it exactly for you so you can send it to your friends. Hope you enjoy the laugh.

Love,
Kimmie

NOW THAT I'M GETTING OLDER BUT CAN'T SEEM TO GROW UP:—

1. I started out with nothing and I still have most of it
2. So I finally got my head together but now my body is falling apart
3. All reports are in, life is officially unfair
4. blessed are the flexible for they will not break
5. If all is not lost, then where has it got to?
6. My attempts to play Badminton are just plain bad
7. It's easier to get older than it is to get wiser
8. I wish the buck stopped here, because I could sure use a few
9. I can't stage a comeback—I haven't been anywhere
10. The only time the world beats a path to your door is when you're in the bathroom
11. If God wanted me to touch my toes, He would have put them on my knees
12. These days I spend a lot of time thinking about the hereafter . . . I go somewhere to get something and wonder what I'm here after . . .
13. Funny, I don't remember being this absent-minded in bygone years . . .
14. If we were really meant to fly in aeroplanes, Jesus would have said, '*HI, I am with you always . . .*' (Matt 18: 20)

With Love from
Kimmie

So I got her back with Mum's Dictionary
Dear Kimmie,
Here's a collection of sayings I found that might make you smile.
Love,
Muz

1. DUMBWAITER the one who asks if your kids would care for dessert after the main meal
2. MY POCKETS handy place for my kids to dump sticky, squirmy or dead stuff they don't want anymore
3. MY SKIRT handy place for my kids to wipe their dirty faces and snotty noses on
4. FULL NAME is what I will always call you when I am mad at you
5. GRANDPARENTS the people who tell everyone your children are wonderful but then add that they're sure you're not raising them right
6. STRETCH is what you guys did to me physically, mentally, emotionally and spiritually even though I was bigger and taller than you.
7. INDEPENDENT how we want our children to be as long as they do everything we say
8. PUDDLE a small body of water that acts like a magnet and draws other small bodies wearing dry shoes into it
9. SHOW OFF a child more talented than yours
10. TOP BUNK where you should never put a child wearing Superman jarmies
11. WHODUNNIT not one of the kids who live in your house

<u>CAZZIE'S 'CHICKEN SOUP' RECIPE</u>
<u>FOR A COLD</u>

If you are unwell with a cold, use the following remedy to help let you get better:—

REST—*is nature's cure*
EAT—*feed a cold and starve a fever*
DRINK—*lots of fluids (chicken soup, water, honey and lemon drinks)*
BE MERRY—*'a cheerful heart does good like a medicine'* (Proverbs 17: 22)

CHAPTER SIX

TRIBUTE TO FANWELL

Before Jim moved back to *Tununu,* he'd been managing for Gerald Turner, another farmer in the area. It was there he'd met Fanwell.

'Fanwell wants to come and work for me here,' said Jim one day. The energetic and efficient bush-telegraph style communications of the African people had informed him of this, and so one sunny summer's day we took the pickup truck and went to collect Fanwell, his wife and all his 'kitundu' (his household stuff). Fanwell immediately impressed me by politely doffing his old bush hat and greeting me with, 'Good morning, Nkosikaas.' It was an old-fashioned address that one rarely, if ever, heard anymore but one of the utmost respect an African man could show a white woman. The more common address was simply 'Madam'. As a tractor driver, Fanwell occupied a relatively important place in the labourers' hierarchy. He was a hard worker, a man whose standard of workmanship was beyond reproach, and he never complained about doing overtime during reaping.

Having said that, though, Fanwell could also be extremely forthright, cheeky even and when the government's 'land-grab' began in 2000, Fanwell was the first to start pegging out lands for himself and other workers on our neighbour's farm. It became apparent that Fanwell's loyalty and allegiance was tilting dangerously towards the 'war vets' who were making our lives so miserable. The last thing we needed was for Fanwell, followed by other farm labourers, to go haring off after them.

'I don't really know what to do with Fanwell,' said Jim one day. 'He's an excellent worker. If I fire him then that will cause even more problems with the officialdom. But he's also causing problems with Mark and I don't want that either.'

Before we could find a solution, however, something happened which radically changed Fanwell's life forever. One day, late in 2000, Fanwell attended our 'compound church' and there he had a life-changing encounter with Jesus Christ. Fanwell pursued that relationship with the same zeal and zest as he put into everything else.

Within a few short months, their Sunday services were lasting all morning and Fanwell also began holding all-night prayer, praise and worship services. He'd always ask permission because the compound, being close to the house, meant that we'd probably be kept awake by their singing. As if we'd mind!

The Lord blessed them by regularly adding to their numbers. One evening, driving home in the golden dust of sunset, we turned into our driveway and passed Africans streaming down the avenue of bohemia trees, laden with exotic and fragrant mauve-and-white blooms, and into our compound.

'Please don't tell me those are war vets,' I was aghast watching them, half expecting some kind of attack.

'I don't think they are,' replied Jim. 'They're too peaceful and relaxed-looking.' He was right. A few hours later, the hymn singing began pouring through our cottage windows.

Soon, Fanwell began conducting services on other farms in the district. He'd regularly come with lists of things he needed for the Church; bibles, hymn books and small teaching books. Like everything else, he put his whole heart and soul into his new life in Christ.

Then came a time of testing for Fanwell, a time when his loyalties to the local 'war vets' were tested. That night came when Jim and I were surrounded by a group of 'war vets' and troublemakers making threats and bent on mischief. We found out later that they had forewarned our labourers that they would be there, and that they were expecting to be supported. When Fanwell and the other members of the Church arrived, they supported us instead. Whilst the air was laden with putrid sour-beer breath, harsh and dark threats of rape and slit throats, they started singing praise and worship songs. Black and white believers side-by-side facing the common enemy.

A few days later we held a service in that same spot. We left it to the young African minister to give the actual service, and I have included his words here also because there was something very powerful about that message. In the subsequent eight years, I have preached that same message a number of times.

The price, of course, was very high for all the African labourers on the farms who may have initially supposed the 'war vets' would naturally include them in the land distribution, but that was a fallacy. The labourers had supported the white farmers voting against Robert Mugabe in the Referendum and there would be no mercy.

Genocide is a terrible illness to spring on people. And as we lost our farm, so all the farm labourers lost everything, too; their homes, their jobs, the plots of land we'd given them. Most of them did not even own a home in the local reserves.

Their future is so very bleak. They will need all the help possible if they are even to survive. Food is being denied them unless they support the country's regime. They are being persecuted in the thousands, if not millions for daring to stand up for what they believe in. They have talents that will never be developed and dreams that will never be realized.

Although many of these Africans are very poor, many of them will readily share what little they do have with others who have nothing at all. They will do what they can to love and support one another. Their motto comes from 2 Corinthians 4: 9; *'We are hard pressed on every side, yet not crushed. We are perplexed but not in despair; persecuted but not forsaken; struck down but not destroyed—always carrying about in the body of the dying of the Lord Jesus Christ, that the life of Jesus Christ may be also manifested in our body.'*

I don't know where you are anymore, Fanwell. I don't even know if you are still alive. I wish I could have told you before we left that I have never before that time or yet since, been privilege to witness such a phenomenal change in the life of a person as I did in yours. And times when my own faith might waver for a short time and I wonder where the hand of Almighty God might be in all of this horror and heartbreak, then I remember your changed life and your courage—and faith, hope and love come back to me once again.

POTHOLES 'BELOW THE SURFACE'

FINAL SERVICE AT TUNUNU FARM CHURCH

'For even the Son of Man did not come to be served, but to serve and give His life as a ransom for many . . .' Mark 10: 45

This sermon is about being taken from slavery to freedom. In old Jewish culture the phrase 'to give as a ransom' was basically the price given to buy a slave. So when Jesus came to give His life as a ransom for many, it meant that He was setting us free from slavery.

In the times that these scriptures were written, there was a tremendous subculture of slavery in existence. In fact there had been a massive explosion in slavery thanks to the rapid Roman conquest of the Mediterranean and there was a glut of slaves to be had. Slave owners could afford to be choosy about who they took on.

There were both Hebrew and Gentile slaves, and naturally the Jews would treat their own Hebrew slaves somewhat better than the Gentile slaves would have been treated. If there were any perks kicking around, the Hebrew slaves would have been first in line. Even so, on the whole, the Jewish nation treated her slaves better than other nations were wont to do. Only citizen classes were considered human. The slave classes were considered goods and chattels.

So the people of the time understood the imagery of slavery very, very well. When Paul used similar imagery in Romans chapter 7 *'For I am carnal, sold under slavery . . .'* they knew what he meant.

Imagine for a moment what it must have been like to be a slave. In the open market places were stands where the slaves stood on display, and above their heads was the sign of the spear. This sign indicated that they were for sale in the slave arena.

Firstly, there was the shame. These slaves were scantily clad so that the slave masters could come and examine them closely. Now if you were young, strong and handsome (like Russell Crowe) you could flex those massive biceps and show the slave owners that at least you were physically superior and as he examine you, you could fleetingly look down on him.

For the rest of the slaves and for women in particular, it could be infinitely more humiliating as slave masters touched their skin and hair to see if these slaves could perform the tasks for which they were being bought. For young women of childbearing age, it was particularly hard, as slaves were often expected to bear children for their masters. These young women, if they were in good condition, could fetch the highest prices at the slave market. Once the price was agreed with the seller, the slave master would take the slaves back with him and he would allocate them tasks.

There was no financial reward for being a slave. Unlike hired men, slaves were not paid for their labour. Sometimes slave masters were good and kind and looked after the slaves they had bought.

In the Old Testament times, according to the Mosaic Law slaves were to be set free in the year of Jubilee, in order to give them a chance to upgrade their status. Some slaves were happy to forego this freedom in order to remain with a slave master throughout their lives. But many masters did not respect what they considered to be lesser mortals. Even in jubilee years, they would release their slaves, only to recapture them all again very quickly, making a complete mockery of the whole system.

Slavery still goes on in many countries today. In Africa there is a greater understanding of slavery, thanks to the Slave Trade that existed for many years before people like David Livingstone and William Wilberforce, together with others, worked with such determination to see it abolished once and for all.

There was the humiliation. If you speak to Africans today, you can hear more about how they were treated. They would be placed on this stand and examined for service. Sometimes the slave master would come with a stick and say to the slave, 'I'm going to throw this stick, and I want you to run and catch it. I want to see how fast you can run and how quickly you'll tire out.' This was because slaves had to be taken on long marches before reaching the coast, where they would be shipped to

America to work on the plantations. So they had to be fairly fit and strong to make the journey.

For the slaves who were chosen and lead away, the slave masters would then warn them: 'You will keep up with this train, because if you fall behind and slow us down, I will have to kill you.' And they would do that, too. They did not want slaves running away and either getting free or getting picked up by another slave master who had not paid for them. Many slaves died this way, and on the crossings as well, because of the terrible conditions on the slave ships.

Imagine even more the humiliation of the slaves who stood on that slave stand day after day, and nobody offered to buy them. A slave master would approach them and say, 'Are you still here? You were here yesterday and the day before that, too! Doesn't anyone want you? How embarrassing this must be for you. Perhaps I will offer the slave owner $2 for you. You aren't really worth it, but hey, anything to save you from this continual humiliation. Then I will take you home and find something for you to do.' This poor slave would probably then realize that he is not long for this world.

Then there is the deep sorrow of being forced away from your loved ones and your homeland. Many slaves who were treated well, who were given good food and adequate clothing and only light duties to perform, still spoke about a 'deep heart pain' that they were never quite able to overcome. They still failed to thrive and sometimes died of a broken heart.

We may not understand these words so well. But speak to someone who has known slavery what he knows about the journey from slavery to freedom that Jesus has come to offer and he will understand exactly what you mean. The disciples, too, would have understood.

As I mentioned before, the slave masters were the ones who chose what tasks these slaves were to perform. Some slaves would become cooks, house servants, vineyard workers and other 'decent' occupations. Others were forced into prostitution and other disreputable occupations. The choice was not theirs to make.

Although we are not slaves in the real sense, there are other ways in which the analogy is accurate. It's not the sign of the spear over our heads that exposes us to the slave market, but it's our sin which acts as the sign of the spear. And that is why we needed the Messiah to come and rescue us. But it cost Him dear as the verse from Isaiah forewarned it would.

Inside 'natural humankind' is the old 'sin nature' that exposes us all for sale in Satan's slave market. When we get caught out in some awful sin, we could excuse ourselves by saying, 'the devil made me do it,' but this statement is only partially true. In one sense the devil cannot make you (or I) do anything, but our sin natures make us vulnerable to his despicable manipulation. Just like real slaves, some people in this situation will become 'decent' slaves; teachers, lawyers, farmers, secretaries or paramedics. They will live in clean and tidy homes with white picket fences and pink rambling roses. They'll have lively children and friendly dogs. But others so exposed in the slave arena will become alcoholics or drug addicts, prostitutes, thieves or murderers. The devil has used his evil wiles to lure them that way. There probably isn't a person on the face of the earth who had a burning ambition to lead such a life. Nobody wants to be an alcoholic; nobody trains to be a drug addict or a prostitute. They have been led that way.

Those of us who were fortunate enough to become 'decent' slaves should never look down on our fellow human beings, because we have all started out life on that same base. We all needed someone to come along and set us free. None of us could do it in our own strength.

Thankfully, whilst we were so shamelessly exposed, Jesus Christ came into that slave arena. He looked us over in love and said to the slave owner, 'I want to take all these slaves. I will pay for them with My own blood. I will cleanse them and clothe them with My righteousness. I will change their status from slavery to freedom. I will turn their darkness to light. I will give them a hope and a purpose so that they may live out their lives in wholesome pursuits. I will give them a goal and a reason to live. I will give them a future. And finally, I will give them a home in heaven.'

Once we have accepted what Jesus came to offer, we are taken off the slave stand. We don't live there anymore. Satan is no longer the powerful, overwhelming force he once was in our lives. His will and purpose for our lives his constant accusations—all are made null and void by the power of the Cross.

There is no shame; we have been clothed with the righteousness of Christ. We live inside the powerful righteousness of Christ. There is no longer any humiliation. God has deemed us worthy of the greatest sacrifice of all time, the death of Jesus Christ on the cross. There is honour in belonging to the family of God. We rule and reign in peace in the heavenlies over Satan and his evil hoards—but he will do anything to stop you from hearing that message or if you do, try and prevent you from believing it. You no longer have to be frightened of him, he is frightened of you. He knows what Christ, living in you, is capable of doing.

Pain and sorrow will eventually be dealt with, as God has promised to wipe away all tears from our eyes.

Jesus' blood has worked a number of wonders specifically in regard to this sin. Firstly it cleanses us and keeps us continually clean as we walk in the light of fellowship. Any sin we commit as believers has already been dealt with. Jesus' blood has broken the power of sin in our lives. Since we are clothed in His righteousness, we are no longer naked, ashamed and exposed to sin as we once were. We can rely on His strength to set us free from its snare. Finally, Jesus' blood removes the penalty of sin from our lives. There is no longer eternal death for someone who believes in Jesus.

Then we go back to the slave stand, the freedom and strength of Jesus Christ and do our 'bit' to set others free. We don't behave like the slave masters and pick and choose the ones we think will do well as believers, we encourage all to see their need and help those who see the true freedom that comes with meeting Jesus, and wanting to be set free, are wanting to reach out in faith.

It is up to us who believe, to live in peace with God and be more than conquerors, just as He promised. AMEN

POTHOLES 'SHORT THOUGHTS'

TREASURED MEMORIES AND
TESTED RECIPES

If you visit the 'Bible Belt' in America today and go into an African-American restaurant, you will find a selection of dishes collectively known as 'Soul Food' and they date back to the days of the trans-Atlantic slave trade.

Slave owners often fed their slaves as cheaply as possible, giving them things like scrap meat and vegetable tops. If these slaves wanted to eat well then they had to do what they could to supplement their meagre rations.

Indigenous crops from Africa like okra, sorghum and rice filtered in, as did cabbage from Portugal, and turnips from Morocco. The slaves began incorporating other local vegetables like cassava, kale, collards, cress, mustard, onions, garlic and pokeweed. Added to the meat off cuts, these crops lifted meals to something better. Later, they began using herbs like thyme and bay leaf giving dishes more zest. They also supplemented meagre meat rations by fishing and hunting small animals and birds.

Forcing men and women to leave their homeland in Africa forever became a death sentence in more than one way. Some died en route and others were treated brutally and life itself was a living death. Even those who were treated well, given only light duties and taken care of sometimes still failed to thrive. All that was dear and familiar lay many miles across the sea and they knew they could never return. They spoke of a 'deep heart pain' that would ultimately cause death.

Slowly traditional dishes emerged and became collectively known as 'Soul Food' because these forlorn, heartbroken people took the dregs handed to them, and put their heart and soul into them in order to make something worthwhile eating. 'Soul Food' together with some of the most haunting gospel music has been borne out of this period of suffering and their lasting legacy has been handed down through the generations.

They pinned their faith on Jesus, believing He had something better for them. They believed that a recipe of hope, baked in the oven of Jesus Christ will transform the simplest, humblest meal into something worthwhile; something tasty, nutritious and filling.

During the season of Lent we tend to give up some special part of our regular meals in order to focus on Easter. As long as Jesus is the reason why we do this; to get closer to Him, to understand Him better, the sacrifice will be worthwhile. This is what we, today, could call 'Soul Food'.

POTHOLES 'SHORT THOUGHTS'

MAKING THE MOST OF MISSPRINTS

I was at work one day when someone showed me this amusing misprint in the paper:—

For Sale: 135 acre farm in lovely setting. Complete with house, barns, arable land and woodlands with wild wife.

We had a good giggle, but when I get hold of misprints like this one, I like texting them onto other people to see what responses come back:

- *Ooh, lucky guy!*
- *Is she for sale also? I might be interested . . .*
- *His wife is wild? He ought to try mine for a weeks . . .*

IN THE POTHOLE

I waited patiently for the Lord;
He turned and heard my cry.
He lifted me out of the slimy pit,
Out of the mud and mire;
He set my feet on a rock
And gave me a firm place to stand.
He put a new song in my mouth,
A hymn of praise to our God.
Many will see, and fear, and put their trust
In the Lord.

Psalm 40: 1-3

A man was walking along the road of life when he tripped and fell into a deep pothole, slimy with mud and alive with frogs, dead insects and a snake. It was too deep for him to climb out of without help.

'Help!' he cried as the snake reared its ugly head. A shadow fell from overhead and he saw a face peering down at him.

The person looked in and said: 'I'm feeling so sorry for you down there in that pit,' and walked on. *That's subjectivity for you*, the man thought, and sighed. The man wondered how many people he'd treated in a similar manner.

Another person came along and briefly blocked out the sunlight. 'It's logical that somebody should fall into the pit. Glad it's not me. And don't worry; you won't be down there forever.' *Objectivity is the better view, but it won't get me out of this hole,* he thought, despairing not only of the pothole, but the uncaring attitude of fellow human beings.

A Pharisee came along and looked into the pit, adjusted his robe and walked on, thinking; *'Only bad people fall into pits. He obviously deserves to be there. Thankfully, I'll never end up in one!'* The man looked up and wondered how that Pharisee had gotten to be a church leader. The Pharisee hadn't even bothered to speak to him!

A mathematician came along next and did a boring calculation about how he'd fallen into the pothole, and summing it up quite accurately said, 'If a giraffe were to fall in there, its head would stick out. Then you must know how deep your hole is.' But he didn't bother to reverse the calculation and figure out how the victim of the pothole would get out again.

'Perhaps you could supply me with said giraffe?' enquired the man, thinking he could at least climb up on its back and get himself out.

'Ooh please could I have exclusive coverage of the story of you falling into that pothole?' asked the next curious head poking over the edge of the hole.

'Are you a journalist or something?' asked the man.

'Yes I am. Just going to get my pen and notebook, so don't disappear. We could get a sensational story out of this.'

A fundamentalist looked in and exclaimed: 'You obviously deserve your pit. You got in there all by yourself, so you'll have to play Solitaire until you can figure out a way of getting out by yourself.' No sympathies there, apparently.

The IRS agent who saw him there asked him, 'Are you paying taxes on your pothole?'

'It's not *my* pothole!' exclaimed the man, getting red in the face.

'Then what are you doing there?' he asked. Rhetorical question really, since everyone falls into a pothole at one time or another, taxmen included.

A self-pitying person slouched up to the pothole, leaned over and told him: 'Think yours is bad? Wait until you've seen my pothole. I've been in it for years and made it as comfortable as I know how. Nobody will join me in mine, of course. At least I don't have to face real life anymore. That's a lot harder.'

The upbeat Charismatic came bouncing along, smiled and said: 'Just confess that you are not in a pothole. Then all will be well!'

His optimistic friend added: 'Things could have been worse. Just imagine what it would have been like if you'd broken your leg on the way down?'

Later, when a pessimist went by he contradicted him by saying: 'Things will get worse. If you didn't break your leg on the way down, you'll break it on the way back up again.'

The man's wild wife (from the previous piece) brought him a plate full of a well-known brand of oven chips and lowered them by rope so he had something to eat. She'd eaten a few of them herself on the way over . . .

The Doctor rubbed his hands and said, 'Oh, goody, another customer. Now let's see what I've got in my bag here . . .'

The wag said: 'It was the short way down and the long way back up again!'

His children said: 'It's your entire fault. We never asked to be born anyway.'

The humourist said: 'Just think what a great story it will make at dinner parties, one day when you get out!'

Above, in the heavenly place where there is complete peace and tranquillity that remains undisturbed by fretful mankind, God the Father knew he would fall into that pit long before he was born and provided him with the most wonderful gift of grace through Jesus Christ—the one gift that above all was provided before he fell it. Jesus would strengthen him and show him how grace empowers him to get out of the pit. 'As long as you know Me, you know what I am capable of,' Jesus told him. *'My grace is sufficient for you. My strength is made perfect in your weakness.'* The man realized that he could do nothing on his own strength to get out of the pit, but suddenly it didn't matter anymore. Jesus was there, to lean down, crush the vile serpent's head and give him a hand to gently lift him out.

Many of us tend to think about it as being someone else's pit and we can think of any one of a number of excuses as to why we don't help people who are in one. It takes us out of our way. It takes time, effort and sometimes resources—all of which we may feel we do not have.

But don't forget that although Jesus can, and sometimes does, supernaturally reach down into someone's pothole and bring them out, He has passed on this Great Commission, this eternal work of His. He works through His people to uplift and deliver those who are lost, cold, scared, hurting or sick. *We* are Jesus' eyes, hands, voices and bodies here on planet earth. Each one of us has the responsibility of doing what Jesus would do and lift the man out.

Psalm 40 gives this wonderful result. The man's feet are placed upon a firm rock, always a great place to be! He is given a new song, a new hymn of praise to fill his mouth. Other people observe the deliverance and in turn they, too, will place their trust in God. Everyone who sees and understands can get together and celebrate by having the greatest party ever. That's what the angels above will also be doing.

MEMORY VERSE: Psalm 27: 5
'For in the time of trouble He shall hide me in His pavilion,
In the secret place of His tabernacle He shall hide me,
He shall set me high upon a rock.'

Just think how happy you would be if right now you lost everything you ever had—and then got it back again!

POTHOLES 'JOY BAG'

:D One of the 'Bible exam howlers' I read recently was: *'The free gift of God is internal life.'* It took me a while to 'see' it because we are so used to reading that the free gift of God is *eternal* life. I do believe there are many who will be very surprised (and overjoyed) to find the gates of heaven opening for them. 'What did I do to inherit eternal life?' they will query.

God will say kindly to them, 'You didn't do *anything*—you simply believed in Me. And that was the only requirement.'

By believing, they already had 'internal' life—and that's what led to *eternal* life.

:D 'I know I am going to hell. That is where I want to be. I'm glad I'll leave behind a system that will ensure most of mankind will follow me there,' *Karl Marx*

:D 'Hell is for Wimps' *Newsboys*

:D Do you believe in Creation . . . or . . . *Evolunacy?*

:D Did God make you a little lower than the angels—or a little higher than the apes?

:D Samson: Lord why did You give me such amazing hair?
The Lord: Because you're worth it . . .

:D One husband, who owned a small country newspaper, took the opportunity to write this on the occasion of his 30th wedding anniversary:-

My wife has been such an excellent wife that this year I'm going to spoil her with a trip to South Africa's 'Valley of a Thousand Hills' where she can spend a month on each hill.

His wife got him back by submitting a recipe for Apple Pie to the newspaper that called for 'one ton apples' (instead of one tin). The recipe was not checked for errors and printed like that . . .

Jonah's song: "Sitting On The Dock Of The Bay" (Otis Redding)

Moses' song: '500 Miles' (The Proclaimers)

Jesus in the desert: "You can go your own way" (Fleetwood Mac) or
"Hey Devil get your junk OUT OF HERE" (Tobymac)

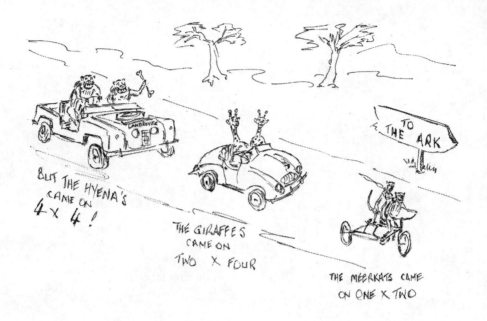

BUT THE HYENA'S CAME ON 4 X 4 !

THE GIRAFFES CAME ON TWO X FOUR

THE MEERKATS CAME ON ONE X TWO

TO THE ARK

Noah's song: "Raindrops keep falling on my head" (B J Thomas)

Paul and Luke in the storm: "There's got to be a Morning After" (Maureen McGovern)

Shadrack, Mesheck and Abed-nigo: "Through The Fire" (Larry Greene)

Nimrod: "Because I'm BAD" (Michael Jackson)

Nehemiah: "We Built This City" (Starship)

The Egyptians trying to cross Red Sea: "Help!" (The Beatles)

CHAPTER SEVEN

WHITE WATER RAFTING DOWN THE ZAMBEZI RIVER

There were eight of us in the raft: one oarsman whose word was law, two girls and five men.

As we approached each rapid, the oarsman would time our entrance, and he would call, 'Ready . . . ready . . . ready . . . HIGHSIDE!' whereupon the people in the front of the raft would hurl themselves forward, and punch the raft through the rapid. That's the general idea anyway, and I guess if it worked properly every time, it wouldn't be classified as a dangerous sport.

You start at rapid no 5 and you end at rapid no 18—so that's 13 rapids in all that you have to get through in a day. That first rapid—that very first rapid I was at the back of the raft. I heard the oarsman shout the instructions, and had one wild second of seeing the guys out in front, suddenly become the guys up above my head, teeter there and then the raft capsized and everything went dark as yours truly came up underneath the raft. Now if you want a truly terrifying experience, try coming up underneath the raft in the dark, churning waters of the Zambezi River.

There is no escape and there isn't a whole lot you can do about it, whilst your are in the rapids, except watch your life flash past your eyes at least a dozen times, before you finally get out and see beautiful sunshine again. We got into calmer waters about three years later, and I 'walked' my hands along the bottom of the raft and got out into beautiful sunshine.

When my buddies couldn't find me, they were panicking about having to tell my folks and my children that they'd managed to lose me on the first rapid!

After that, our oarsman lined us up along one side of the raft and showed us how to push down hard on it, to make it flip back over again. After each rapid, all the kayaks and rafts would wait until everyone was through safely before pressing on. The day we went there were 17 rafts and 5 kayaks.

Once everyone was through, we were off, jabbering with fright for the next rapid. This wasn't so bad—we didn't flip but I did get thrown out of the raft. It was so quick I didn't even realize I was out, until I heard the oarsman saying something like, 'get her in quickly.' We were heading towards a big rock face at high speed. You are not encouraged to stay in the water longer than necessary, because of the crocodiles that also like to do white water rafting. There's nothing quite like the sight of a crocodile leering at you open-mouthed from the bank to get you back into the raft very speedily. It's a bit like looking into a cave of teeth!

And then there are the steep sides of the escarpment towering up on either side of the gorge, a mass of lush tangled undergrowth far too thick and sides way too steep for even the most hardened bundu basher to climb up it. Once you are that far down the Zambezi gorge there is no other way of getting out except via the river. And it's a long, long way to the climb out after Rapid no 18.

Rapid no 8 is the longest of all the rapids, but we managed to get through that without any hitches at all. Then rapid no 9 is classified as a 'Grade 6' rapid and therefore, by law, too dangerous for the public to go through. You have to get out of your raft, and carry it around the rapid on the rocks. Some of the oarsmen took the rafts through on their own, but I suspect that the rafts, being a lot lighter like that, were a bit easier to get through.

There were three rapids in a row, which weren't too scary, so the oarsman decided to put us two girls in the front and the men in the back. Each time he yelled, 'Highside' we'd throw ourselves over the front of the raft, and we'd hear a chorus of men behind us all laughing. Being quite cheeky, I did eventually turn around and challenge them with a "Scuse me, but what's so funny?'

'Ah, it's the delightful way your bottoms come up in unison every time you do that!' they replied, wiping their eyes.

All this time though, you are made aware of the fact that the last rapid no 18 is always the worst, short and sharp with just one single massive wall of water to be got through. Most of the rafts capsized on this one, but I am grateful to report we got through just fine.

Then, with the rafting over for the day, you still have not finished. There is still a long climb up out of the gorge—something like 300 stone steps and you have to carry everything with you.

When you get to the top, you're exhausted, but there is someone standing there with a bottle of cool drink in one hand and a beer in the other, and he says, 'which one would you like?' And that was the best cool drink I have ever had.

In the evening you all gather at one of the hotels, because the kayaks have been going through the rapids filming everything that happens, and they put together a video of your day, and you all watch it together. It's really quite festive with a lot of camaraderie, cheering and a bit of teasing. You've challenged the elements together and you've won. It's like a real victory celebration.

Despite the fact that it is a dangerous sport, on the whole, only about two or three people a year are actually killed, so the mortality rate is very low.

I think life in Zimbabwe was like that. The fast-track land resettlement program that started in 2000 was like being thrown through the rapids. There were times when the violence and hostility would become very active, and then there were times, when like the quiet pools, it would die down. The 'war veterans' would visit regularly, but apart from a lot of threats, there wasn't much action. And then it would start up again.

Yet through it all, it was as if Jesus is always the oarsman, who doesn't take us out of situations, but who gave us the necessary commands about how to get through them.

We were all had a part to play, and in order for us to get through the situations we were in, team work was of paramount importance. That in itself brought about the kind of camaraderie that always brought about a special kind of love and giving, and allowed us to keep a sense of humour and quite often see the funny side of things. Yes, there was an incredible sense of belonging to a group of people who really cared about one another.

The raft itself is like the Holy Spirit, holding us together just above life's circumstances. The courageous Christians would be in the front, working together as a team to get through the dangers, and the ones in the back—well—they were also part of the team and they weren't going to get left behind. They were cheering on the leaders out in front, giving moral support and stability to the fairly flimsy raft.

Part of being a Christian is knowing and trusting through all of life's circumstances, that God is not just the God of Good Times, He is the God of All Times, good and bad.

Finally, He challenged me with a hymn we used to sing with great gusto. We had been in England, I think only a few days when the words of this hymn kept running through my head: *He who would valiant be, 'gainst all disaster* . . . and the Lord spoke to my heart and said to me something like, 'Think of all the times you have sung that hymn with great gusto during the good times and for you, the words were true. Now that disaster has struck, are the words still true?' I hope we have all, as a family risen not just to this challenge, but to several others which also somehow invaded our lives.

In 2001, just a year into the Land Invasions, it became increasingly clear that we were up against another serious problem. Timothy, my youngest, became increasingly ill. He'd developed a swollen knee years before which had been diagnosed as 'Viral Synovitis' and he'd told to rest as much as possible for a couple of years. Mission Impossible for an active, lively youngster who always preferred being somewhere on the vertical, rather than horizontal, plane, he'd been a keen gymnast and rugby enthusiast, hurling himself with wholehearted energy into everything. When he started becoming active again, he ran cross-country and did really well, but soon developed a swollen ankle. The knee we knew was not the result of an injury, having been checked over by a Doctor who specialized in sports injuries. He was the one who'd told us it was 'a-traumatic' (illness rather than injury) but the ankle we assumed was an injury. But as the weeks passed, it did not heal.

Timothy's overall health deteriorated but several Doctors could not give us any reason why. Blood tests for Arthritis came up negative. Then suddenly, more joints swelled, and his back, shoulders, elbows all became swollen. Timothy couldn't hold a cup of tea or open a car door, he was so weak. I was so thankful to Dr Stilgoe who finally gave us the diagnosis of Arthritis, because at least we now knew what we were up against and Dr Gunning, the Specialist who devised state-of-the-art treatment. He spent his first few weeks of Form One bedridden, on a small dose of Methotrexate (in higher doses, it is used to treat cancer patients) and steroids which prevented him from sleeping for a few years but it did all get Timothy onto the road to recovery.

Timothy is a one-of-a-kind, unique person who never allowed the illness to get the better of him and he devised his own ways of coping. If he couldn't play active sport, then he joined the First Aid club so that he was still a 'team player' travelling around with St George's rugby team and helping to man the First Aid Tent. He also joined the shooting club and made the most of his time in other ways. He learned to eat healthily and which supplements would aid the road to recovery, to overcoming and finally, victory. Along the way, he taught us a great deal about courage, coping with life's curved balls and how to get the best out of every situation.

Robin had struggles, too, with chronic back pain, but the diagnosis was different. A number of tests indicated that there was some asymmetrical development in the spine. He worked hard to overcome the pain. He studied hard and passed exams and even returned to Africa for a time, working as a missionary.

Kimberley developed asthma and anorexia nervosa. When we arrived in the U.K. in 2002 we had two chronically ill children and a very small support network, but God's people are everywhere and kind-hearted Christians in the south of Devon reached out with sympathy and goodwill, helping us in many ways and praying for our beleaguered family. After a few years, Kimberley too, fought the condition and learned to be an over comer in her own right.

Not all the youngsters were able to do so. Tragically, a number of their friends unable to cope with the trauma of lawlessness, committed suicide and our hearts go out to their families, always.

We have seen them, in a way, reliving the days of our teenage years. Not in a 'liberation struggle' or 'bush war' (depending on whose side you were on) where we had law and order, police and army backup and were allowed to carry weapons, although violence and killing were the order of the day. They have experienced life in a context of lawlessness and total lack of security, where remarkable courage and self-control have been displayed instead of retaliation. They have seen that lawlessness in all its ugly reality thrive in an atmosphere of state-sponsored violence and the resultant devastating trashing and loss that must always occur in its wake . . .

They have finished out their growing years away from the farm, in another country far from the one we call home. So have their cousins Carly and Tammy, as will many other friends, who are now scattered all over the world. When and if they return, the things of childhood will have gone. As adults, I wonder what they will find, what they will think and where it will all lead to.

Here in the beautiful south of Devon, Jim was given the wherewithal to retrain as a Plumber sporting his cheery 'Hippo' logo on a van that also sports stickers representing all his training; Gas Safe Register, Oftec Licence, Rayburn and AGA, Worcester-Bosch Boilers, plus 24-hour emergency call-out. I took up working in an Independent Living Scheme with Special Needs youngsters, who have taught me a great deal. I hope to return one day to see Melan who is living in Harare, visit family and friends and just remember the good times when this was my country, my home and my life. Like the Jews of the Diaspora we have learned to live in another country. Praise God for His empowering grace, all He has taught us, all He has given us, so many blessings we still can't count all of them.

POTHOLES 'BELOW THE SURFACE'
'WHAT DO YOU WANT ME TO DO FOR YOU?'

'Feel this, Barties,' Abigail instructs. I can hear the sharp crackle and smell the acrid smoke, as Abigail spreads out my fingers to the melting warmth. It seeps into my fingers, mellow and soothing.

'That's the colour red,' she states.

'So red is hot, crackly, and acrid-smelling,' I say.

'Colours don't make sounds or smells,' Abigail giggles. It's a game she likes to play with me. She pulls me up by my hands and plunges them into a large jar of water. The warmth disappears abruptly.

'Ooh, that's cold,' I mutter, feeling the elusive liquid slipping through my fingers.

'It's blue, same as the sky.'

This dear, sweet little sister of mine tries so hard to make blindness a better place to be. And she has this marvellous way of describing things, developed over years of persevering. Thanks to her patience, I've been able to build up some idea of what things should look like. Having been blind since birth, I have absolutely no idea and the concept of colour is particularly elusive. Abigail refuses to give up and has created a whole unique world in which I live. Sometimes it bothers me, these places I cannot go: colours, the inner courts of the temple, marriage, my own home and wife, earning a decent living.

Abigail pushes a small bowl of fish and a tiny loaf into my hands and leaves me to eat in peace whilst she goes outside to feed the chickens and water the gourds.

'Come on Bart. We need to get you to Beautiful,' Abigail bustles in, pushes my stick into one hand and takes the other in one of hers and together we go through the streets of Jerusalem to the city wall and the gate called 'Beautiful' where I would spend the day. Here I am an equal amongst beggars, others who like me, have some form of physical disability. I know who they are by the sound of their voices and the smell of their sweat. They're a good bunch and we talk about life; each detail of which requires endless discussion.

Abigail slips away and I begin to assess what sort of a day I'll have by the atmosphere around me. The 'red' people are warm and compassionate. They give gifts to several of us beggars. The 'blue' ones are cold, callous and indifferent. They give nothing except, possibly cruel words.

'It's either your fault or your parents' fault that you've ended up where you are. We all get what we deserve.' It's this knifing assessment from total strangers that really pulls me down.

It isn't so much the lack of sight that really bothers me. After all, I've never had it and one cannot miss something that has never been a part of our lives. It's this set-apartness that comes from this sense of being the dregs of society, the beggar, and the family member who's let the other family members down by exposing the sin. The temple's inner sanctum denied to me for life, for all of my life, because I am deemed 'unclean'—God just beyond my reach, on the perimeter fence of my life. For no one who's ever been born blind has found a way to see.

But today I sit in the sunshine and it feels good. I listen to the discussions of others when another sound begins to penetrate my thoughts. It's growing steadily louder. It's the buzz and roar of a teeming crowd and it sounds as though they are coming this way. A wave of tense excitement precedes them.

'What's going on?' I ask Thomas who is sitting beside me. He half rises and wobbles a bit.

'I think it's that strange healer man and the hordes that always follow Him, but I can't get up to see.' His frustration is evident. He feels the same way about being crippled as I do about being blind.

'Quick, Thomas, climb up on my shoulders. I can walk and you can direct my footsteps, and together we can find out about Him.' My heart was quickening in a strange way. A healer? Here? If only we could get to Him! Thomas doesn't hesitate and I stagger under the unaccustomed weight.

'We may end up collapsing in a heap,' Thomas informs me, wriggling a bit to get comfortable.

'As long as the heap's at His feet! Come on, Thomas. Every second's going to count.'

'He comes from Galilee and He's healed people this past . . .' but I've heard enough, like a sudden revelation that my whole life I'd been waiting for this moment.

'I want to see! I want to SEE!' I shout, but the sound gets sucked into the crowd. I don't know exactly where He is, but there's no other way of attracting His attention. Thomas starts shouting, too. Our voices mingle.

'Oh shut up you fool. He isn't interested in a blind beggar like you,' I hear those ugly words from someone in the crowd. But for once I am too desperate to take any notice. Everything inside me rebels against these harsh, loveless words.

'Put me down, Bart. He's here.' Thomas shouts the words right into my ear.

Someone takes hold of my hands. The skin is rough but the touch is gentle. They are the strong hands of a young man. I didn't know who He was but I had the strangest sensation that all the colours were flowing from Him simultaneously, separate and distinct, seamless and smooth, timeless from years long past to those yet to come. Each colour passes through me and stirs something deep within my soul. I don't know why, but I count each band as it moves, passing silently through me. There are seven altogether: red, orange, yellow, green, blue, indigo and violet like the regal robes of wealthy people. They blaze a trail of brightness, hope, gaiety and laughter, warmth, healing and cleansing, beauty and splendour, majesty.

Then they swirl and mix together and there is a surprising sensation of white hot light; burning, encompassing, and engulfing me entirely. Holiness. For a moment outside of time there is complete tranquillity. This is peace beyond anything I have ever known.

The white-hot light splits again, this time into just three: blue, red and yellow. They're there, each one ministering to me in a distinctly separate way and yet it makes a blended whole. The blue one pierces a lifelong sense of depression. I've had it for so long that I'd ceased to think of it as anything but normal. In its wake, joy bubbles out. The focus shifts to yellow and I'm engulfed in warmth. It's flow is smooth and penetrating deep inside, descending from my head all the way down. It's smooth, soothing as oil and fragrant as cedar.

Then comes the red. Blood. I realize what it is and am at once repulsed and yet drawn by the desperate need of it. It's warm and sticky and pulses with complete and supernatural healing.

Without warning, everything is withdrawn and in the sudden absence the darkness within me, for the first time ever, is complete.

How long it lasted, I do not know. I was only aware of my painful need of it. Involuntarily I cried out in the direction it had gone.

'What do you want of Me?'

The crowd had tried to hush me but they didn't know. Nothing was going to make me stop. The yearning in me was hot and rolling.

'Master, I want to see! I want to see! I want to see all that again!' Everything is ripped wide open inside me and the desperate plea I could never bring myself to admit, not even to myself.

Then came the blessing, the turning point as He said, 'Go your way. Your faith has made you well.'

I never did go my own way again, choosing instead to follow Him all the way down the dusty road to Jerusalem, and beyond, a decision I never regretted.

I'm old and well spent in years but unafraid of the fearsome power of death because that, too, was overcome a long time ago at Calvary. My wife, Rhoda, looks after me as well as Abigail once did, before she married and had children of her own. I enjoyed my own two children and six grandchildren who have all in turn filled my home and my life with their chubby laughter and amusing ways.

Thomas and I visited the temple only once that week before the horror of Calvary. After His resurrection, we never went back again. There was no need, for His Spirit is everywhere.

We sit outside our own homes, small as these dwellings are, they belong to us. We sit in freedom in the sunshine and still have long discussions about the tiniest details of our lives and the strange events of the past. I'll never forget Thomas's temerity, when shortly after my own healing he turned to Jesus and enquired, 'What about me?' Jesus smiled, touched him, and the weakness had gone, never to return. That day when Thomas climbed on my shoulders to be my 'eyes' while I acted as his 'legs' was the most outstanding and we've enjoyed the wonderful, lifelong changes which have been ours ever since.

POTHOLES 'SHORT THOUGHTS'

PRAYER SHIELDS

'. . . *Above all taking the shield of faith with which to quench the fiery darts of the wicked one . . .*' Ephesians 6: 16

In the list of spiritual weapons for spiritual warfare, the shield Paul was talking about was long and rectangular just about the size and shape of a door (from which it takes its name.) For a properly trained, strong and alert soldier, this shield was the complete defensive weapon that kept him protected from all the missiles of the enemy.

It's interesting to note that the breastplate of righteousness (Ephesians 6: 14) and the breastplate of faith and love (1 Thessalonians 5: 8) and the shield of faith all do a similar job with one important difference.

The breastplate of faith and love serve primarily for our own purposes, our own defence. The large shield of faith is there for the protection and provision of all those whom God has entrusted to us. It will be big enough to cover everything, trust Him!

As we wield the shield of faith to parry all the fiery darts of Satan, also pray and claim the protection of the covering of the blood of Jesus over yourself and your loved ones; everything that is important to you. As we step out in faith, the enemy will look for any fiery dart he can hurl at you. He will do anything to stop you from understanding the true message of grace. You need to wield that shield of faith with determination and precision.

A group of soldiers together wielding these large shields could form a 'phalanx' and could advance on the enemy's territory, each soldier not only protecting himself, but the soldier next to him also. So the grace that Jesus gives us is not only a personal anointing, it also prepares and empowers us to be part of the body of believers to which we belong.

Each prayerful, powerful member of a family, fellowship or Church needs to be united. Unity is the one thing Satan is most afraid of and he will do anything to hurt or damage our unity. Don't give him the opportunity. Unite, become part of a phalanx and advance on the enemy's territory.

MEMORY VERSE:-
Joshua 23: 10
'One of you puts to flight a thousand, since it is the Lord your God who fights for you, as He promised you.'

THE BATTLE BELONGS TO THE LORD.
JUST YOU, ON THE LORD'S SIDE, IS STILL A MAJORITY!

<u>POTHOLES 'SHORT THOUGHTS'</u>

<u>WHAT DO I HAVE TO GIVE?</u>

The crippled guy was begging by the gate called Beautiful just as he had always done; his expectations reduced to looking for offerings that would ease his sufferings but he found out one day that Jesus Christ looks on the heart of the problem—the deep healing he desperately needed. Think of the true freedom which would be his then!

When we look at the intense sufferings of those around us, we can focus on their immediate needs and our slender resources . . .

. . . silver and gold have I none

. . . room in my home I have none

. . . eloquent speech I never had anyway

. . . and I don't always possess a sympathetic ear

Or do we, like Peter and John, see the immediate need, the real need and look to the Greatest Resource of All? *'I have no silver or gold, but what I have I give you; in the name of Jesus Christ of Nazareth, stand up and walk.'*

Jesus had taught them, *'Freely you have received, freely give.'*

Here were the two apostles doing just that, passing on the miraculous healing in the power of Jesus' name, and the man who had never walked, was walking and leaping and praising God!

Some years ago a young teenaged girl, I'll call her Chantal, really enjoyed her sport. She was 'into' every sport the school had to offer and excelled at sports. Then one day she became crippled through a debilitating illness and eventually had to use a wheelchair to get around. Bravely, she still attended sports matches, as a spectator, to cheer on her teams.

One day, whilst in such a position, the veil between this world and the unseen realm was opened before her. An enormous, bright angel was shielding her whilst brandishing a 'firesword' and he simply said one word to her: *RUN!* Without questioning whether she was capable or not, she leapt out of her chair and fled! She never went back to that chair but regained complete use of her legs and went back to playing sports. This time, however, she went round various Churches and Christian groups sharing her testimony and passing on the Good News that Jesus Christ is still in the business of miracles today, praise God!

Have you ever experienced the immediate presence of God that brings about an amazing miracle? If you do you will discover a well of the deepest, sweetest joy that will have you embracing a fullness of life you never knew existed! You too, will leap about, unrestrained and filled with joy and you won't mind if the whole world knows!

As freely as you have received, so freely pass on to those who don't have, not just the temporal blessing of physical healing, food or clothing, but the eternal blessing of coming into God's family. And then just let go and have the greatest time ever celebrating all that He has to offer!

MEMORY VERSE:—
Matthew 10: 7, 8
'. . . *And as you go, proclaim the good news, "the kingdom of heaven has come near." Cure the sick, raise the dead, cleanse the lepers, cast out demons. You have received without payment. Give without payment.*'

ALWAYS BE A CHANNEL OF GOD'S BLESSING AND NEVER A RESERVOIR

POTHOLES REFERENCES

'Zimbabwespeak' is made up of a colourful mixture of languages including English, Shona, Ndebele and Afrikaans. The words I used in the course of this book:—

Gomo's—hills
Takkies—tennis shoes
Guti—cool, misty, damp and overcast weather which usually blew north from South Africa
Toppies—Layards Bulbuls, or Black-eyed Bulbuls

Obrom Boop-pants—fairly harmless, just very ugly corn crickets

Vooping Birds—Fantasy Birds courtesy Bill Eckert

Blaas hoppies—puffer fish

Bundu Bashing—exploring the bushveld

Shuteen or gwandashas—other words for 'bushveld' but usually more rougher, thicker and designed for the more rugged individuals who enjoy getting torn to shreds, full of thorns and splattered with unnameable muck

Vellies—bush shoes designed for aforementioned rugged individuals

Claylaggies—a game played with flexible sticks and lumps of clay by seriously foolish people

Picanins—African children

Catties—catapults. Ours were never the shop-bought variety. Usually made from forked sticks and rubber from old tractor tyres and anything else creative people could remove from the farm workshops

Ah,Ah, Iwe—scornful Shona term usually reserved for recalcitrant children or other badly behaved individuals. For Zimbabweans living in the Zimbabwean Diaspora, do have a T-Shirt with the words *'Ah, Ah, Iwe!'* printed on it. Wear it when you want to go 'Zimbabwean Spotting'

Mampara—similar to *Ah, Ah, Iwe* only several degrees worse

Chegubu—plastic container

Chibuku—African beer brewed from sorghum

Sadza—traditional African food made from dried, ground mealies cooked into stiff porridge and squashed into balls, dipped into relish and eaten with a lot of lip-smacking enjoyment

Shosholoza—traditional African song that will raise terrible fear in all your opponents (with the possible exception of the All Blacks performing the haka)

Gobbie—new soldier with very short haircut

'Cookie boysa lo scoff'—Cookie, please bring the food

Bush War or Second Chimurenga—the same Rhodesian war (it just depended which side you were on as to what you called it)

Terrs or Gooks—Terrorists

Shamwari—friend

Braaivleis, braaing—outdoor cooking of meat over an open fire

Grawb—someone you didn't like

Troopie—soldier

Sam's Drag—Samora Machel Avenue (running through Harare)

Sissies, wussies—weaklings or other fearful individuals
Bundu—bushveld
Smaaks—likes fancies
Kitundu—clothing
Gogomannekie—type of African lizard which has a sense of humour
Nkosikaas—old fashioned Shona term (very respectful) for the lady of the house
Nunu's—insects
Baas—Boss
Shuparing—bothering
Wovvits—'war veterans' or other hostile people trying to take your farm by any means possible, but usually resorting to hostility and violence, lawlessness and mayhem, chaos and complete senselessness
Toy-toying—a dance Africans do when they are angry.
Basopa lo hubcaps—mind the hubcaps
Datenda—thank you

WITH SPECIAL THANKS

There are, as always too many people to thank when it comes to life's experiences and what you learn from them. Most of them are mentioned somewhere in the book, and each person you come across in these pages is a real, live person. Some of the names or identifying characteristics have been changed purely for reasons of privacy. I love them all.

I'm including a letter here from Peter Lorimer, not only because it is special to me, but also because it is indicative of the love and fellowship we shared with so many people—and fellowship is the end purpose of the gospel. We are called 'out of Egypt' and 'into fellowship' with Jesus Christ and we become members of another family. I am so privileged to be a part of that family.

To all the young people who were part of Highlands Presby Church in those days and each of whom came to mean so much to me. Special thanks goes to Andy Vaughan for asking me to join 'Yadah' and for trusting me enough to set up such a team. What treasured memories! Also to those who were part of The 'C' Team and whose love and valuable input did so much to help so many people. There were others like James Buckley, who is responsible for so many people joining the ministry; Laura Rouse, Phil George, Ed Campbell, Donnay Downey who gave of time and talents to help out. Donnay, we never did get to visit Lalapanzi, but hey, maybe one day. Keep it on the cards, okay? Thanks also to others who filled our days with joy and made sure we were never lonely; people like Brian McDonald, Quentin Tannock, Tony daCunha, and Russ Harrison whose capers definitely need to find their way into print!

Thank you to Jim's family for welcoming myself and the children into the family and to friends I made in Tengwe. Oscar and Leeann Johnson and the whole Johnson clan, Rory and Debbie Richards, Tim and Laurie Dawson, Paul and Leigh Boddy, Jan and Tessa Kageler, Mark and Wendy Letcher, the Hays, and many others who'd shared Jim's life for the whole of his lifetime, but who I got to know in difficult, traumatic circumstances. We were thankful to see Mike Mason when he came to visit us here in the U.K. before he died so suddenly. Despite the fact that he's mentioned here purely in comedy, on the serious side, he also did a huge amount to help struggling African people.

I'd like to make a special mention to the ones who didn't make it through: to the victims of Viscount's *Hunyani* and *Umniati,* to John a courageous Captain and his Co Pilot Garth Beaumont for landing that crippled aircraft. I'd also like to dedicate it to my lovely friend Jenny Elliott and her daughter, Sarah. I have a photograph of Sarah sitting at a small table outside in the sunshine eating lunch with Kimberley and Robin. Sarah never made five years old. Mother and daughter died together on the treacherous ninety degree bend in the road after it passes through the small town of Chivhu. To Andy Shaw whose preaching I still remember fifteen years later—so straight down the line, so to the point, and so powerful. Also to Preston, Dudley and Daniel—all youngsters who impacted my life in some way and whom I will always remember: like Fred, you were just too young. Not long after coming to the U.K. we were walking around the beautiful English church where Rob Haarhoff now ministers. The afternoon sun was steaming multicoloured and warm through the stained glass windows. Along the walls were Remembrance Plaques dating back many years. One of them had this beautiful dedication:

> *Where he is, there is peace.*
> *Time is not, nor is there*
> *The slightest sorrow*

And we cried as we thought once again of you all and trust that you are all safe and comforted in the everlasting arms of the One who cared for you more than we ever could. One day we can all sit in the warmth of God's eternal sunshine together and none of us will be older than 33. For in heaven we are eternally young; the ageing process is something that is related to a fallen world only.

Thank you to all our labourers, again too numerous to mention; John and Beauty, Edward and Anna, Ostar, Philip, Leo, Makangira, Bauleni, Zondiwa, Babbiton and of course, Fanwell. You were our great supporters; you were the ones who made Tununu Farm thrive into what it was and you who lost everything at the hands of your own kind. There is a terrible price always to be paid at the hands of an angry dictator. I'd like to add a special note to David Kasere who worked so hard to achieve so much. I wish I knew where you all were now—but then again, I may find it too heartbreaking.

Once we'd arrived in England, too, there we found God's people for they are everywhere. A special thanks to Arthur and Sheila Worrall, Rod and Debbie Hardwick, Dave and Monica Chapman, Grant and Trish Camilleri, Dave and Cyndi Botha, Adrian and Timmy B, all of whom shared our pain and gave us courage, hope and strength. And Adrian, of course, who 'won' every argument until I turfed him out of the room and when I'd calmed down and he instinctively knew when re-entry was safe. Eventually we came to understand each other really well. Thanks to the 'Facebook' team through whom we made contact with so many people of our own Zimbabwean Diaspora and who we never thought we'd see or catch up with again. Thanks to FB we found Chris and Geraldene Saint and have more happy memories now in the U.K. Again, there are others too numerous to mention but the fellowship shared has been wonderful. We would never have made it without you guys. Thank you also, to the people whose sayings I have used in this book and whose names don't appear anywhere. If anyone knows their names, please feel free to pass them onto me.

One final thanks to other writers who have made such a difference to me: Barbara Johnson's 'Spatula Ministries' who is my inspiration for this book. A great lady whose courage still amazes me and whom I wish I had met. Also to Francine Rivers, Philip Yancey, Robert Farrar Capon and especially to Joseph Prince for their 'Grace' writings and teachings—all of whom who have given me a greater understanding of what Grace is really all about. I say 'especially' to Joseph Prince because I discovered his teachings at a time when life once again became a hearbreaking catastrophe and I wondered if I'd got it all wrong. Thanks to Pastor Prince, I found my way again and I hope to pass it onto others, too. Thanks also to Newsboys and Tobymac whose music lightened many a dark tunnel and brought light at the other end.

Yadah Memories by Peter Lorimer

I have been racking my brains, to try and pick special Yadah group memories. There were so many, it was actually quite difficult to pinpoint.

My most special memories were away from the group, with just you and I having heart to heart chats, that is where our friendship became really close.

With that bond made, it became easier for you to entrust me responsibilities I treasured greatly, such as leading the worship group. The highlight being our carol service which I fittingly titled 'Carols at Carols' where I asked members of the group in a random order to share what Christmas meant to them, in between chosen carol favourites. I remember it being one of the most vulnerable, raw, open and yet healing and refreshing times as a group, as people spoke about little robins and snow, children's fantasies and Jesus Christ demonstrating what He had come to die for, and not so that we could give each other presents. I remember not being the only one to shed a tear that evening.

I remember being able to use my time away at YWAM, to do some real growing up of my own, and sharing the insights with the group on my return, in particular a fresh view on the full armour of God, with which you were most impressed. Also, being able to lead discussions out of my favourite book (yet to find my own copy, but one day I shall) 'Poet and Peasant' by Kenneth Bailley and using my 'A' Level English knowledge to its absolute limit.

I remember two teaching tapes you organized for us from Africa Enterprise, the one is a bit hazy but it concerned a terminally ill lady who encouraged people who, while not being able to be in the theatre with her, could still be in the waiting room. The other was the testimony of a guy who survived the Teneriffe air disaster, who didn't suffer a scratch or burn, or even the smell of smoke on his clothes, whilst every other passenger in the seats around his were burnt beyond recognition, recognizable only by the resume at the Arrivals desk.

I remember two specific outreaches we covered, to Prince Edward Senior school, where we heard the powerful testimony of the Head Boy, and took great encouragement that the school was in good hands, and the outreach at Chinhoyi High School, which was Andy Vaughan's farewell gig, where I was asked to pray in the circle at the end, for the fruit of the message and for Andy's future. I remember people starting to giggle as the prayer broke the five minute barrier, but I just felt so convicted in the Spirit to pray through certain areas that I just carried on. (We still made it back to Harare before sunset!)

Finally, I am thankful for the friendships that have stood the test of time, since the group went its separate ways. The fact that we are in touch with Chris and Geraldene, Alannah, Chris and Alaine, Maurice and Jo, Charlie and Lynne, Andy and Lynne, Mike Southall, Mike Jeffries, Ed Campbell and last but by no means least, Lawrence Trim on Facebook, whilst Richard Wakefield was around for my wedding.

When you and I had our lowest moments, we somehow managed to bump into each other and share away our troubles. The fact that you also trusted me to Housesit in Northwood for you, and knew that you could rely on me to travel out to Banket with you at all hours of the morning and bring the kiddies back in time for school (I would have travelled to Tengwe with you, at midnight if necessary!).

'There is a time for everything, and a season for every activity under the heavens'

Ecclesiastes 3: 1

Seasons come and go, but bonds formed remain forever. The Counselling group was your vision, and I count it a privilege to have been a small cog in it's workings.

Peter Lorimer